A Manual for Trustees

Of Colleges and Universities

By

Raymond M. Hughes
President Emeritus
Iowa State College

Third Edition

THE IOWA STATE COLLEGE PRESS • AMES

PREFACE

This book is the result of a conversation with Mr. John W. Hobbs, of Toronto, president or director of a number of large Canadian corporations. He spoke of the great importance of the policy-defining duties of the directors of corporations and of the diverse loyalties which tended to pull the president of the corporation in different directions in an endeavor to serve patrons, employees, and stockholders.

In thinking of this discussion and applying the conclusions to college and university presidents and trustees, the book developed. Dr. W. R. Boyd, chairman of the Finance Committee of the Iowa State Board of Education, did much to encourage me to develop these ideas and put them in final shape.

Having served for sixteen years under the trustees of Miami University and for eight years under the Iowa State Board of Education, and having served for three years on the Board of Directors of the Presbyterian Theological Seminary of Chicago, I have observed the operation of trustees both from within and from without their membership.

In writing and developing this material, I am deeply obligated to Dr. John H. Powell, then instructor in History and Government at Iowa State College, now Associate Professor of History at the University of Delaware, with whom each section was discussed in detail and by whom the original manuscript was critically read. The last three chapters were suggested by him and outlined in conference with him.

The first draft of the manuscript was read by Dr. W. R. Boyd; President Emeritus Frank L. McVey, of the University of Kentucky; Miss Anna Lawther, of the Iowa State Board of Education; and Mr. Walter Coles, President of the Board of

Trustees of Miami University. Each of these friends made suggestions and comments which contributed materially to the development of the material here presented, and I am under much obligation to each of them.

Preface to the Third Edition

In this new edition, an effort has been made to bring the various tables as nearly up to date as available figures make possible. Numerous changes in the text have been prompted by advances in administrative methods.

The rather surprising demand for a book addressed to such a specialized group as college trustees astonishes me. But from my own personal acquaintance with the problems of trustees, I am conscious of how important their office is and how much depends on the way they fill that office.

College trustees are usually able men, but many defer too much to the president and fail to use their judgment in college affairs. They must leave administrative detail to the president and are right in doing so, but on general policies they are as capable of forming correct judgments as the president, and here their obligation is great. I have tried to emphasize this point and to give some suggestions which may be useful to a newly-appointed trustee.

The times are difficult for all education. Education—and particularly wisely-administered higher education—is more important to our country than ever before. I hope this book may carry a useful message to many trustees.

RAYMOND M. HUGHES

March, 1951

TABLE OF CONTENTS

PREFACE v

FOREWORD ix

SECTION I. THE TRUSTEES AND THEIR RELATIONS TO THE OTHER GOVERNING AGENCIES OF COLLEGES AND UNIVERSITIES

1. The Selection and Appointment of Able Trustees   3
2. Three Governing Agencies—Their Duties and Responsibilities 11
3. Overlapping Interests and Conflicts of Authority   19

SECTION II. THE SPECIFIC RESPONSIBILITIES OF TRUSTEES

4. Property and Finance 30
5. The President and His Appointment 38
6. The Responsibility of the Trustees as a Court of Appeal 48

SECTION III. THE RESPONSIBILITIES OF TRUSTEES IN DETERMINING POLICIES UNDER WHICH A COLLEGE OR UNIVERSITY IS ADMINISTERED

7. Background for Considering Present College Problems 50
8. Enrollment, Admission Requirements, and Limitation of Numbers 61
9. The Campus and Buildings 73
10. The Scope of the Work of an Institution . . 76
11. The Faculty 85
12. The Library 114

13. Daily Chapel 123
14. Scholarship and Student Activities 125
15. Intercollegiate Athletics 132
16. Fraternities and Sororities 135
17. College Residence Halls 140
18. Placement of Graduates in Employment, and Alumni Relations 143

SECTION IV. The Need for Looking Ahead

19. Each Institution Should Seek Its Own Proper Level 150
20. Common Aims and Goals 155
21. The College and the Individual 162

SECTION V. The Duties and Services of Trustees

22. The Duties and Services of Trustees 170

INDEX 175

FOREWORD

Fifty years ago even our greatest colleges and universities were rather small in size and simple in organization. Today even the small colleges are rather complicated organizations. The great majority of the 1,000 or 2,000 college trustees, newly appointed each year, regardless of background, or breadth of education and experience, will find many problems brought before them of which they know little or nothing. An effort is here made to put together in brief form the generally accepted policies and practices relative to the more common problems which arise in college administration, in the hope of enabling trustees to act more effectively and of magnifying the importance of the policy-fixing duties of trustees.

SECTION I

The Trustees and Their Relations
to the Other Governing Agencies
of Colleges and Universities

CHAPTER 1

THE SELECTION AND APPOINTMENT OF ABLE TRUSTEES

OUR colleges and universities are among our most important and most permanent institutions. They are important because they are the chief centers for the discovery of the truth, for the preservation of knowledge and for the advanced instruction of our youth. Their permanence can be appreciated by considering the Universities of Oxford and Cambridge in England as contrasted with the church, another permanent institution. These two universities were founded nearly a thousand years ago, when all English people worshiped in the Roman Catholic Church; later they flourished under the English Established Church; at present they contribute leaders to many of the dissenting churches, and continue to grow amid increasing sects. Today these universities are stronger and more influential than ever before. They play a permanent role in the cultural life of Great Britain.

The growth of attendance at our colleges and universities is evidence of the increasing confidence of our people in their work and service (see Table 1).

Today the large majority of our able youth attend college, and many influences are at work to bring about the attendance of all youth of marked ability. In the near future almost all of our leading citizens will be college trained. All professional men and women must now prepare in college and professional school. Most research workers, of whom we require a rapidly increasing number, are trained in the graduate schools of our universities. Increasingly, industry and business are directed by college-trained men.

TABLE 1
GROWTH OF COLLEGE ENROLLMENT

	College Students	Percentage of Youth 18–21
1880..............	44,594*	1.06%
1890..............	123,135	2.39%
1900..............	237,592	4.01%
1910..............	355,213	4.84%
1920..............	597,880	8.14%
1930..............	1,100,737	12.37%
1940..............	1,494,203	15.60%
1950..............	2,535,265	26.90%

* About 15,000 more were enrolled in attached academies or were engaged in subcollegiate work.

Although we hear criticisms of these institutions on every side, many of them fully warranted, the faults and weaknesses are largely traceable to the magnitude of the task, to the enormous increase in the number of students in recent years, and to the great difficulty of training youth for the life of today and at the same time fitting them for a profession or other occupational career. The demands for special training are steadily increasing.

The Importance of Able, Interested, and Well-Informed Trustees

Our colleges and universities are a necessity of civilization and must be maintained regardless of religious, political, economic, and social changes.

The final control of these institutions resides in the trustees, regents, directors, board of governors, or whatever the controlling board is called. The quality of their service depends largely on the character of the members of the boards and on their active concern for the institutions under their general direction.

There are in the United States about 1,880 separate institutions of higher learning. While some boards control several of these Institutions, in general each institution has a separate board.

The number of trustees on each board varies from 5 to 100. Probably the large majority of boards are composed of 9 to 27 members. There are probably 18,000 to 25,000 persons on governing boards for institutions of higher learning in America. Their effectiveness, their competency to discharge their duties, and their full understanding of their responsibilities are important. Too often they merely serve as official rubber stamps of approval of the acts and recommendations of the president of the institution. The purpose of this book is to clarify the duties of the board of trustees and the duties of the president and of the faculty, and to show how an effective board can contribute most largely to the highest service of the institution it controls. It also attempts to outline the policies relating to many aspects of college and university administration that have generally proved to be sound.

Influences Affecting the Selection of Trustees

In view of the importance of these institutions to our civilization, it is most desirable that they be directed wisely and administered ably. The ideals and character of the faculties of these institutions, the quality and inspiration of the teaching, their adaptation to the current needs of society, their general efficiency, and their adequate support depend very largely on the trustees. It would seem that only the very best and ablest citizens available should be appointed.

Unfortunately, this is by no means the uniform practice in public institutions; too often men are appointed for political reasons. These are sometimes merely unimportant and useless people. Often they are highly injurious to the institutions, introducing political prejudices and pressures into the control of educational institutions. On the whole, however, the men and women on these boards are capable, conscientious, and deeply concerned to serve usefully.

In private institutions, members are often appointed because of their wealth, their prominence, or their supposed influence in securing money for the institution. Too often such hopes are disappointed. Appointments should be made with the purpose of securing the ablest persons available who will devote a reasonable amount of time and thought to the institution.

Most institutions have on their boards at least a small group of able, devoted trustees generous of their time and thought. Such are invaluable. The entire board membership should be of this type.

The Appointment of Trustees

Usually the trustees of public state institutions are appointed by the governor and confirmed by the state senate. In some cases, as at the University of Michigan, they are elected. The trustees of a large proportion of private institutions are self perpetuating—new members are elected by the board itself. In many church colleges part or all of the trustees are appointed by the proper church authority. In some institutions part of the trustees are elected by the alumni. While other authorities appoint trustees in some cases, the great majority owe their positions to election or appointment by one of the above authorities.

The appointment of trustees is usually for three, five, six, seven, or nine years, or for life. In public institutions an effort is usually made to frame the laws so that no one governor in two terms can appoint a board majority and so gain control.

On most boards there are too many old men. The average age of the members of a given board is very often too high. It would seem desirable to keep the average age between 50 and 60. It would also seem desirable that no member should serve beyond the age of 70 years. There should certainly be a substantial number of members between 30 and 50 on these boards.

It seems more important that the board should be young enough to sense the needs of the people they represent and guide the changing institutions to their largest service, rather than that a large majority of aged men should maintain policies unchanged.

The membership of the board should certainly include some alumni of the institution and a majority of members who are college graduates. Some members of the professions are desirable. The members should broadly represent the classes of people the institution is designed to serve. Farmers should be represented on boards of agricultural colleges; engineers on boards of engineering schools, etc. Newspaper editors often make very valuable contributions.

A study of the occupational activities of the members of nine state university boards of trustees in 1944 showed that on the average a board of nine members included three business men, three lawyers, one editor, one homemaker, and one doctor, farmer, or teacher.

Real devotion to the cause of education, profound concern for the public good, sterling integrity, courage to face pressure, political and otherwise, fearlessly—these qualities combined with high intelligence and some knowledge of higher education should be prerequisites to the consideration of a man or woman for appointment.

The President of the Board

While much is said and written about the president of the college, we hear very little about the president of the board of trustees. Just as the college never rises above the level of the president, so the board rarely rises above the level of its president in observing faculty rights, in planning for the future, in fixing policies, or in being independent of political or other outside influences.

While the function of the president of the board is entirely different from that of the president of the college or university, it means everything to have the best possible man in this post. Outstanding courage is a prime requisite. All kinds of matters come to him that need courageous handling. In a state institution a governor is often tempted to interfere in the operation of the institution. He has no authority or right to influence the institution in any way except as he nominates trustees. Should he suggest anything along other lines, the president of the board should be able and ready to fully defend the independence of the board.

In the same way there are board members who are tempted to interfere in the running of the institution by suggesting appointments, dismissals, and other matters to the president of the college. These misguided individuals can be controlled only by the president of the board.

Besides these problems many more arise that a courageous and independent president of the board can and should settle. Among these, the merchant who wishes his wares bought by the college regardless of price or quality, the parent who demands special privileges for his child, the citizen who wishes a job for his protègè—all these come eventually to the president of the board of trustees.

Many men who are presidents of boards of trustees fail to recognize the magnitude and possibilities of the position they hold and merely act as presiding chairmen, rather than as leaders.

It seems very unwise to retain a man as president of the board until he becomes really old. After serving under two old men in the above capacity, the writer realizes how largely their usefulness is decreased by age. It seems probable that no man should serve as president after he reaches 70. The danger lies in retaining a man so long that everyone is afraid to suggest his retirement. At the same time everyone wants to protect him from worry and difficult problems, and the result is that for years the institution is deprived of the active protection and leadership of a well-led board of trustees.

In reading what has been said above about the president of the board and of many other matters in this book, the reader probably will recall instances where the suggestions here laid down have not been observed and where an institution has survived and prospered. It is essential to remember that a college or a university is full of life and energy. It is very complex, and each part retains much vigor. It is difficult to destroy it by mistreatment, and it survives much mismanagement. It would probably survive even if the board of trustees ceased to exist. The purpose of this book is to suggest how the trustees can operate to *best* advance the interests of the college, to serve most generously the youth who comes to it for an education.

Meetings of the Trustees and Their Committees

The meetings of boards vary greatly. Large boards of small institutions usually meet once a year and handle interim business through committees. An executive committee ordinarily has several meetings annually in such a case, and other committees meet as required.

Where the membership of the board is small, from five to twelve, there is a strong tendency to have more frequent meetings, to reduce the work of committees, and to handle a larger proportion of the business by the board as a whole.

It is the general opinion that a board of from seven to fifteen members is preferable to one larger or smaller. If the board is too small it is difficult to maintain on it a sufficiently wide representation of the people, and there is danger of the board members becoming too active in the detailed direction. On the other hand, as the board is increased above twelve or fifteen, it is hard to maintain its entire membership with persons of as high a type as is desirable, and with larger numbers the sense of responsibility of individual members decreases.

While the titles of committees vary, certain functions are usually covered by committees. In the case of large boards an executive committee almost invariably acts during the interim between board meetings. Most boards maintain a committee on buildings, a committee on finance, and a committee on education and faculty. An inspection of catalogues discloses a great variety of other committees determined by the needs of the several institutions.

Probably the ideal board would have seven to twelve members; would meet from four to ten times a year, depending on the size of the institution and the amount of its business; and would maintain committees on finance, buildings, and education and faculty.

In the early days, as the institutions were all small and as there were few expenses aside from professors' salaries, there was very little business for the trustees to consider. Often very large boards were appointed with a view to spread widely knowledge of, and promote interest in the institution. These boards met once a year. Now with much business of importance before every board we have a very different situation. A small group, the members of which are really interested, who will attend meetings regularly, and who fully grasp the problems of the institutions, is ideal. Their problems are very similar to those of a board of directors of a business corporation.

With the large board fixed in the charter or by-laws, it is difficult to reduce its size. This situation has usually been met by delegating large power to a small executive committee which meets often and transacts the major business of the institution. The board as a whole meets once or twice a year to approve the actions of the executive committee and do such other business as is referred by the executive committee.

Some boards are split up into a number of committees, each having large authority within certain areas, and each reporting to the board as a whole.

CHAPTER 2

THREE GOVERNING AGENCIES—THEIR DUTIES AND RESPONSIBILITIES

IN THE days prior to about 1875 there were only three bodies of authority in an American college—the trustees, the president, and the faculty. As colleges grew in size and wealth, further administrative officers were added: the dean, the registrar, and the business officer—variously called business manager, treasurer, bursar, secretary of the board.

In the present usual organization the business officer represents the president in business matters, the dean represents the president in educational matters, and the registrar keeps all academic records.

The trustees hold all property, authorize the budget and budget changes, fix policies, appoint the president, and serve as a court of final appeal in all matters.

The faculty, under the board, teaches all students, determines all curricula and courses to be offered and all classes to be taught, and assigns classes to teachers, determines grades, who shall graduate, and who shall receive degrees, both in course and honorary.

The president is the chief executive officer of the board of trustees and also of the faculty. With the aid of the business officer, on the one hand, and of the dean, or deans, on the other, he is responsible for the administration of the educational and financial affairs of the institution under the policies and regulations set up by the board and by the faculty. Depending on the interests and talents of the president and immediate needs, he may devote his chief efforts to financial or to educational problems.

The control of an institution in all its parts is shared by the board of trustees, the president aided by the chief financial officer and deans, and the faculty. Their several spheres of authority are fairly distinct but overlap in places. Some consideration of the chief loyalties of each of the above agencies will throw light on their duties and their limitations. It is important to recognize that any authority is limited by its loyalties (see Table 2).

TABLE 2
THE CHIEF LOYALTIES

of Trustees	of President and Officers	of Faculty
to Legislature or Donors to Parents to the People	to the Trustees to Legislature or Donors to the Faculty and Staff to the Students to the Parents to Alumni to the People	to the President to the Dean to the Individual members of the Faculty to the Students to the Trustees to academic standards to the academic standardizing agencies

It has been the aim to arrange the loyalties (Table 2) in the order of their influence. Others might arrange them differently. Theoretically, perhaps the first loyalty of each of these agencies should be to "the truth." Undoubtedly each is deeply concerned with the discovery and preservation of the truth, but this is an abstract loyalty, and each of those listed in Table 2 is quite concrete.

Very briefly, the functions of the above agencies are as follows: The trustees control all financial and property matters and determine general policies. The president administers the institution under policies fixed by the trustees. The faculty controls teaching and research and is responsible for academic standards. These duties will now be amplified.

The Duties and Responsibilities of Trustees

The loyalties of the trustees are simpler and less personal than those of the president or faculty, and their duties are

more general in nature. They stand between the institution
and the public. It is their responsibility to see that the types
of service for which the institution was established are rendered as effectively and as economically as possible, and that
as many properly prepared students as possible are adequately
served. It follows that the chief duties of the trustees are to
determine policies and see that these policies are carried out
by competent administrative officers.

The policies controlling the scope and operation of a college
should be fixed by the trustees with advice from the president
and the faculty and should continue with slight modification
from administration to administration. The trustees and not
the president should determine what sort of an institution
they control. Too often we see the whole policy and personality
of a college changed by a new president who reorganizes it in
accord with his own ideas. Certainly the president should
feel free to suggest changes in policy, and the trustees should
give his suggestions careful consideration, but the fact remains
that the control of policy is a function of the trustees and one of
their most important functions. It is also one of which they
very often lose sight.

It is highly desirable that the policies of the board be published in pamphlet form in sufficient numbers to be distributed
to the faculty and alumni. This should be republished when-
ever revisions of consequence are made. Such a publication
would give the faculty and alumni increasing confidence in
the board of trustees.

When the trustees overlook their function of determining
policies, they tend to become an official rubber stamp of the
actions of the president. It is rather their duty to assure
themselves that the president's administration conforms to the
policies laid down by themselves.

In addition to determining the policies of the institution,
there are three very important functions of the trustees usually
fixed in the laws governing the institution:

1. The trustees hold title to all property and are custodians of all property of the institution.
2. The trustees are responsible for the appointment of the chief executive officer of the institution, ordinarily designated as the president.
3. The trustees constitute the final court of appeal of students, alumni, faculty, and all staff members, who feel that the administration has not adequately cared for their interests.

The Trustees and College Business

It is always highly desirable that no trustee have any business relation with the college. He should in no case, directly or indirectly, sell anything to the college; insurance, supplies, bricks, stone, or anything. Often it is suggested that trustees can sell certain items to the college more cheaply than they can be bought on the market. This is sometimes true, but the saving is bought at the high price of the independence of the college business office. In public institutions business relations of trustees with the institution under their control generally are prohibited by law. It should always be prohibited by the rules of the trustees themselves. If such relations once become established, they cannot be broken off by the president or business manager of the college, since these men are employees of the trustees, and no fellow trustee can protest without implying distrust of the integrity of his fellow member. The only safe relationship in a business way is absolute exclusion of every trustee from any business relationship transactions with the institution.

The Duties and Responsibilities of the President

The president is the chief administrative and executive officer. As the representative of the trustees, it is his duty to see that the institution is operated in conformity to the policies fixed by them. As chief executive officer, he is finally responsible for everything concerning the institution and for the effective and economical operation of all departments. He is responsible to the parents for the well-being, good conduct, and education of all students. He is the chief adjuster of all difficulties which are brought to his office and should discover and adjust many difficulties before they reach the stage when they must be brought to his office. As the executive officer of the general faculty, he presides at meetings, and with the assistance of the deans he is responsible to the faculty to see that their regulations are enforced. The president recommends to the trustees all appointments, promotions, dismissals, and salaries. He is often occupied with the general public which comes to him for assistance and with criticisms and complaints. His duties are numerous, and all of them should be discharged in conformity with the policies approved by the trustees.

Perhaps no better statement of the functions of the president has been made than that of Charles W. Elliott of Harvard, in his inaugural address in 1869. "However important the functions of the President, it must not be forgotten that he is emphatically a constitutional executive. It is his character and his judgment which are of importance, not his opinions. He is the executive officer of deliberative bodies in which decisions are reached after discussions by a majority vote. Those decisions bind him. He cannot force his own opinions upon anybody. A university is the last place in the world for a dictator. Learning is always republican. It has idols, but not masters."

While of course he always should be free to suggest to the trustees new policies or modification of old policies to suit the times, the president should not himself fix policies but leave this for the trustees.

The responsibility of the president is so to administer the institution that these policies, fixed by the trustees and faculty, are faithfully carried out, or to submit recommendations for changes to them. Appointments to vacancies and new positions are to be made so that they will contribute to the effective operation under the fixed policies. Appointments must be made with a view to best serving the students and also to carrying out the aims of the institution in research and scholarly achievement as fixed by the trustees. The president must be loyal to all staff members and guard their interests as to tenure and salary and in every other way. It is his responsibility to see that deans, department heads, and all in authority are of a type and ability to render fine leadership to those under their direction. He should concern himself with guarding and promoting the best interests of the students. He also has responsibilities to the alumni, supporters, and friends, to maintain the spirit and morale of the institution. His position is often rendered difficult when some of these several loyalties conflict, as when the alumni press for a stronger football team than the academic standards and the integrity of the institution permit; or when the trustees desire a department discontinued to which the president has appointed a staff which depends on its continuance for support; or when the salary demands of able men call for salaries above the scale adopted by the board.

Recognizing the fact that the president must operate under a variety of more or less conflicting loyalties, the trustees, when they feel compelled to take action affecting staff members, should always allow sufficient time for execution, so that adjustments to the change can be made without serious injury to anyone.

The formal duties of the president may be listed as follows:

Attends meetings of trustees and reports periodically.

Recommends the annual budget and any later necessary changes.

Recommends appointments, promotions, dismissals, salaries, and salary changes.

Presides at meetings of the general faculty.

Represents the institution before the public.

Represents the institution before large donors or before legislature.

No complete list of his duties can be made. The president is, or should be, the chief servant of all, always willing to help student, professor, employee, or any others needing his aid in their work or trouble. His authority is considerable, and he can be the most helpful man in the institution.

The Duties and Responsibilities of the Faculty

The faculty includes all members of the teaching, extension, and research staffs. In a small college there is only one faculty. In a university there may be quite a number. Usually, faculties of Arts and Science, Medicine, Law, Education, and a graduate school are included. In addition there may be faculties of Theology, Engineering, Commerce, Agriculture, Home Economics, Dentistry, Pharmacy, and others.

The general faculty in a university usually is made up of the permanent members of the entire teaching and research staff who under the regulations of the institution have the right to vote. Often the younger members also attend but do not vote. In some institutions with large faculties, one hundred members are elected by the faculty to represent them, and a more workable group is secured for action. The president presides over the general faculty. Each school or college faculty is presided over by its respective dean.

All matters directly connected with teaching and research are under the control of the faculty. Matters of common interest to all are determined by the general faculty, and matters wholly within the interests of a particular college are determined by the faculty of that college.

The faculties, within the limits of the policies of the trustees, determine what courses will be taught, fix the requirements of each curriculum, fix the passing grade and the requirements for graduation. They vote all degrees, both in course and honorary. All rules and regulations affecting the work and conduct of students are fixed or approved by the faculty. All examinations are set by members of the faculty or by persons selected by them, and the grades given are final and not subject to revision by any administrative officer.

Inasmuch as the whole purpose of the institutions under discussion is to give instruction to students and conduct research, it is easy to see that possible conflicts in authority can arise.

CHAPTER 3

OVERLAPPING INTERESTS AND CONFLICTS OF AUTHORITY

Trustees and President

WHILE the trustees undoubtedly have the entire institution under their control and can take action on any matter, it is with few exceptions most unwise for them to act on any detail of appointments or administration. The president is their executive officer. It is his duty, and he should be entirely capable to handle all the detail of administration. Any encroachment on his authority in detail by the trustees usually makes serious trouble. Trustees are frequently asked for appointments to the staff or for college business. All such requests should be referred to the president without recommendation. The trustees should confine their action wholly to determining policies and controlling the finances. If the president does not administer the college acceptably, his resignation should be called for, and a new and acceptable administrator should be appointed.

In some cases the president arrogates to himself authority that belongs to the trustees, and here again trouble results. Certain decisions about the physical plant, the campus, and the design of buildings, letting of contracts, and construction of new buildings definitely belong to the trustees. The president on his own authority sometimes decides matters of this kind contrary to the ideas of the trustees and puts himself in an embarrassing position. Occasionally, a president announces a new policy which has not been approved by the trustees, and if it is questioned by them, either the trustees must acquiesce or the president must withdraw his announced policy with resulting embarrassment.

It will save much misunderstanding if the president keeps the trustees fully and promptly informed about all developments of any interest at the college. It always annoys a trustee to receive the first news of an occurrence of which he should be informed from an outsider or through the columns of a paper. The president and trustees should always be in complete accord.

There is much advantage in the president sending a multigraphed letter to each trustee monthly. Such a letter would contain *all* news of concern to the trustees and would keep them in close touch with all happenings at the institution. Such a letter protects the trustees from ignorance and misinformation about many minor matters, and it necessitates the president keeping close track of occurrences of possible interest to trustees.

The President and the Faculty

In order to understand the friction which sometimes occurs between the president and the faculty, it is necessary to consider the development of our institutions and the difficulties that grew as their size and complexity increased.

Prior to 1875 the president was usually the only officer, and the faculties were small. With very few exceptions faculties numbered less than thirty, and expenditures outside of faculty salaries and fuel were very small. No laboratories existed. All business of every kind was settled around a table at which the faculty members sat under the president as presiding officer. All business was determined by a majority vote, and everything was most democratic.

As institutions grew and developed this procedure broke down. Students and faculty grew to unwieldy size. Business increased in amount and complexity. Business officers, a registrar to handle records of grades and degrees, and deans to deal with students and educational detail, were appointed to assist the president in handling his growing problems. While faculty members did not wish to devote more and more time to administration, they were reluctant to see less democratic methods prevail. Today most friction between the faculty members and the president is due to a feeling on the part of the former that the president has acted autocratically in one or another matter without duly consulting them.

We now have institutions with more than 3,000 instructors teaching more than 20,000 students and with annual expenditures of more than 35 million dollars. With the multiplicity of matters for decision, it is increasingly difficult to always consult with faculty members and carry on in a democratic manner.

However, some things can be done which go far toward satisfying the faculty in these matters. How far these policies can be carried out in any institution must depend on the decision of the president and trustees. The following policies would generally be very acceptable to faculty members.

1. In institutions of more than 5,000 students, appoint a Provost or Vice President with full authority over all faculty and curriculum matters, appointments, salaries, etc. This will greatly relieve the president and will give the faculty greater access to the man in authority.

2. Authorize the faculty to elect by ballot a committee on committees, which will nominate members of all committees of the faculty.

3. Authorize the faculty to elect by ballot a small committee on administration to represent the faculty in all or part of the following matters.

   a. To take up with the president any matter concerning a member of the faculty.

   b. To consult with the president on any administrative matters, including the budget and salaries.

   c. To represent the faculty in a joint committee of trustees

and faculty in the nomination of a new president, when
that office becomes vacant.

d. To meet with a committee of trustees of equal size to
discuss common problems.

4. The faculty of each college desires the privilege of electing
its dean or participating with the president in the selection.
Where the Dean is elected, it should be for a term of 4 or 5
years.

5. All members of the staff appreciate easy access to the
president's office to discuss with him any matter they desire
to bring up. If the opportunity is wide open, the number
who take advantage of it in any year is not great. However, deans and department heads usually disapprove of
such direct easy access, except for themselves, and insist
that all matters go to the president through them. It must
always be difficult to choose between the advantages of
each plan.

The president is daily pressed with unanticipated problems,
all calling for decisions. Usually matters come to him only
because they are beyond the authority of minor executives.
Most of these matters are within his authority and clearly
under policies fixed by the trustees which properly call for his
decision. Among 100 such matters there is always a number
which should best be referred to a department, to a faculty,
or decided after conference with one or more professors. The
president himself sometimes acts on matters really calling for
faculty reference or consultation before he thinks of the
desirability of faculty consultation, or because he is pressed
into a quick decision by circumstances. Each such failure
to consult faculty opinion before action is called autocratic
and results in criticism of the president. Usually, the president throws himself open to the charge wholly without inten-
tion. However, every such occasion is unfortunate, and the
wise executive will err on the side of consulting the faculty
too much rather than too little.

It is vital that the president and trustees remember that every faculty includes a large proportion of members who know vastly more about their respective fields and matters relating to them than do their board or president. These men rank high among their professional associates in the country. Their opinions are highly esteemed by their equals. They cannot but be astonished and hurt when matters which touch their interests are decided without themselves being consulted.

They feel that they constitute the essential part of the institution—the teaching staff. They and the students *are* the college. If they are regarded and treated as hired men, employed to do a task and to be dismissed when it is done, they resent it. Unless they feel that they are taken into full cooperative fellowship by the president and trustees, are regarded as fully worthy of confidence, and are consulted largely on all plans, they cannot be happy in their relations or do their best work.

This does not mean that college professors are temperamental, or especially sensitive. It is simply the nature of the enterprise. If, in a given institution, a professor is not vitally important in all matters bearing on his field and work, he is not important at all, and the position does not attract him.

In general it may be safely concluded that those institutions render the finest service in which the faculty members are happiest and most contented in their work. One important basis for such contentment is the feeling that their opinions in the fields of their interests are esteemed and sought by the president.

The Provost or Academic Vice President

A new and important movement has been initiated in a few large institutions in the appointment of a man to carry the burden of matters pertaining to education, academic appointments, and the curricula. In at least 50 and probably in 100 of our largest institutions this addition to the executive staff could well be considered. The pressure on the president to give attention to numerous insistent matters steadily increases. The most time-absorbing matters which he can put aside to gain time relate to education, since these matters are the direct responsibility of deans and department heads. So, as our larger institutions are generally organized, the most important interest of the institution—education—is first neglected by the president, when under the pressure of other matters.

The title of this new office has not yet been confirmed by practice. Provost, academic vice president, executive dean, dean of the faculties, vice president in charge of education— all have been suggested or used. The title is rather unimportant, but two things are essential to make the appointment of real value. The incumbent must have the large confidence of the president, the deans, and the heads of departments; also he must have extensive authority in his field.

In practically all colleges and universities today an officer is in charge of business and finance. In a number of institutions, especially in large universities, this officer has been made vice president in charge of finance and business. These men have large independent authority, but keep in close touch with the president through frequent conferences when all important matters are discussed. This procedure should relieve the president of all concern about most routine business matters and allow him to concentrate on such important financial problems as especially need his attention. This same policy should be pursued with the academic vice president. Through frequent conferences the president should be kept informed of all important matters and all appointments under consideration, and should make clear his own views so that the vice president can properly reflect them.

We certainly have 50 or more institutions now so large in

staff and so diverse in the scope of subjects taught, that the right appointee to this post could much more than earn his cost by raising the quality of men appointed to positions each year. In each of this group of institutions there are from 5 to 15 deans or directors and from 40 to 75 department heads. These 45 to 90 persons are directly responsible for appointments, curricula, teaching efficiency, and research in their respective fields, but anyone with college experience knows how greatly they differ in the knowledge, vigor, judgment, and conscientiousness with which they pursue these matters. Some can be relied on to do all that can be done; others, many others, need the cooperation of some higher authority to press them to secure the best results. An academic vice president, thoroughly familiar with the staff, competent to deal with educational matters, and free to devote all his time to this work without interference from external matters, could be most valuable. He should certainly be protected from demands for speeches before general audiences.

Further, and this is most important, the policy suggested above of appointing an academic vice president would materially broaden the field from which a president could be selected. Hitherto it has been essential to select a man familiar with college procedures through experience as a professor and college administrative officer. If a man is added to the staff who will be responsible for appointments, curricula matters, and the quality of teaching, the selection of a president need not be limited to the above group. In the president we need rare qualities of personality, sympathy, and understanding together with high qualities of leadership, a sound sense of proportion, and high ability as a creative thinker. If assisted by an academic vice president on one hand, and by a financial vice president on the other, the lists of persons to be considered for president may well be extended to include clergymen, lawyers, and businessmen, as well as deans and professors.

The Appointment of Deans and Department Heads

The method of these appointments varies with the institution. In the most democratically administered the deans and department heads are elected by the faculty concerned. In some institutions these appointments are made by the president and trustees without any consultation with the faculty. Between these extremes middle courses are followed, where the president, after more or less consultation and advising with the faculty, makes these appointments.

For these appointments to be successful the appointees must have the full confidence of both the president and trustees, and of the faculty members under their jurisdiction. To secure such confidence on both sides close collaboration between the president and faculty is essential, whether the initiative is with the one or the other.

Any faculty ought to have members on the staff capable and suitable to fill these posts. When appointments can be made advantageously from staff members, it is usually simpler to secure general approval. When it seems necessary to bring in men from outside, it is both more difficult to be certain the appointee is the type of man desired and also to assure agreeable cooperation.

It is certainly desirable to consult the faculty members concerned fully, or to turn the initiative over to a faculty committee on which the president or dean sits as a member.

Honorary Degrees

Most institutions confer a few honorary degrees each year on distinguished citizens whom they wish to recognize. It is the privilege of the faculty to nominate the recipients of these honorary degrees to the trustees who have the final approval or disapproval.

All degrees in course are voted by the faculty and are

concurred in by the trustees as a matter of form. Honorary degrees are different, inasmuch as they are conferred wholly in honor of past services and accomplishments of the recipients. Occasionally trustees are inclined to press the names of men for honorary degrees from personal friendship or in an endeavor to secure financial aid for the institution. In no case should a trustee go further than to suggest the name of a candidate to the faculty, with whom the formal nomination lies.

Honorary degrees should never be conferred to win favor. They should be conferred only on men and women who have won recognition in their professional or public services.

SECTION II

The Specific Responsibilities
of Trustees

CHAPTER 4

PROPERTY AND FINANCE

THE responsibilities of the trustees fall into two groups: those usually defined in the charter or legally assigned to the trustees, and the responsibility for determining policies. A discussion of the first group follows.

Holding Title to Property and Responsibility for Finances

In the great majority of institutions the title to the property of the institution—land, buildings, and equipment—is vested in the corporation or board of trustees. In some state institutions the title is held by the state. Legally, the trustees would seem to be personally liable for this property, but so far as the writer has been able to learn, no trustee has ever been forced by law to make good losses of endowment or other property.

As we analyze this responsibility we see that the property of an institution usually consists of:

Land
Buildings
Equipment
Endowment
Current Income

The responsibilities relative to each of these items are considerable and of several types.

Land. During the early years of higher education in America, many institutions originally holding considerable land relinquished title to much of it through the failure of the trustees to foresee the growth and development ahead. Other institutions, had the trustees reasonable foresight, could have secured the additional land demanded by later development at a very small cost. Later this land either cost a great deal or could not be obtained. The wisdom and foresight of trustees in securing and retaining adequate and suitable land for the ultimate growth and development of an institution is of fundamental importance.

Both residence and business property are attracted by the very nature of a college campus, centering the life of hundreds or thousands of students and staff members; by the permanency of the institution and the campus; and by its inviting prospect. A campus is quickly surrounded by buildings that are expensive to acquire and that are not readily available. It seems strange that more colleges have not acquired land in addition to an ample campus, and profited by its sale.

The trustees are responsible for fixing a wise policy relative to land.

Buildings. The trustees are responsible for types of architecture, design, structural perfection, and maintenance of buildings. They select architects, approve plans, let contracts, and are responsible for the honest execution of contracts. They are thus responsible for all unsightly, inadequate, poorly planned buildings, and for poor construction and unwise location. They are responsible for all building equipment and for proper maintenance of buildings, their equipment, and insurance. Of course most of this in detail will be executed by others, but the responsibility is the trustees', who should satisfy themselves that proper action is taken in relation to all building matters.

Equipment, books, and supplies. The trustees are responsible for adequate provision of equipment, books, and supplies. In our forty largest institutions, the amount invested in these items varies from about one-tenth of the investment in buildings to nearly one-half. In the majority, the investment in these items is from one-fourth to one-third of the cost of buildings. Naturally the larger the institutional interest in science and technical education and research, the larger the investment in equipment. The more closely the institution is limited to a liberal arts college, the smaller the needed investment in equipment. Adequate provision is highly essential to effective work and for the contentment and efficiency of the staff.

It can well be remarked here that while the laboratory sciences are now usually well supported in funds for equipment and supplies within the resources of the institution, the equally desirable expenses of nonlaboratory departments, especially history, economics, and sociology, are often overlooked or inadequately provided. While these departments do not require laboratories in the ordinary sense, they need funds for travel to their source material, for considerable clerical work, and for other essential purposes. The staff members in these fields cannot but be distressed and annoyed to see the needs of the science departments well provided, while their equally needed expenses are ignored.

Endowment. The responsibility of the trustees for all funds accepted as endowments is peculiarly great. The integrity and business-like care of endowment funds should be one of the first concerns of trustees.

It by no means follows that all money offered an institution as a gift should be accepted. Gifts toward the general, unrestricted endowment are always welcome. But all gifts for the endowment of special causes, enterprises, or interests should be very carefully scrutinized. Any specific endowment may, after some years, cease to serve a useful purpose. If so, the board is embarrassed how faithfully to handle its trust. Every effort should be made to build the general endowment and to discourage specific endowments. Usually special current needs could be as well served by a direct gift, usable over a relatively brief period of years, while the need is relatively certain, than by a permanent endowment.

During the recent depression many endowments were used in part either for current expenses or as security for loans to be used for current expenses, both uses wholly out of harmony with the trust involved when an endowment is accepted. There is almost no more serious charge that can be brought against a college board of trustees than that the endowment funds have been in any way jeopardized or lost.

Each trustee should assure himself that every possible precaution be taken for the safety and preservation of endowment funds. The competency and integrity of the person or persons charged with investing and re-investing endowment funds should be of the highest. Regular, fully detailed and easily understandable reports on all such funds should be made, and all such reports should be competently audited.

The trustees are responsible for a policy that will fully safeguard all endowment funds.

Current funds. The collection and disbursement of all current funds and all accounting is usually in the hands of the business manager. He is variously styled treasurer, secretary of the board, comptroller, etc. It is increasingly common in our larger institutions to find the business manager entitled vice-president, in charge of business. In our larger institutions a large staff, supervised and directed by several highly trained and experienced men, is required to handle the current business. For most effective operation all business should be headed by one man who, under the president, has entire charge of all business operation and of the physical plant.

The selection and appointment of the chief business officer is second in importance only to the appointment of the president. An able man here can relieve the trustees and the president of worries about finances and about innumerable petty details. He can materially increase the income and through careful buying reduce the expenditures. To be most valuable the appointee should be primarily a business manager. Too often a banker or an accountant is appointed to this office who, while able in the field of his experience, is not really competent to direct to the best advantage all the many business operations of a college. The business of a college or university has come to be as specialized as that of a bank or other distinct business field. It involves collections, accounting, and investing; purchasing, building, operating, and maintaining a large plant; managing dormitories and boarding halls.

It is most desirable to secure as business manager a man who has already gained successful experience in such operations at another institution. Such a man who is fully equal to his job, whose integrity is above question, and who works agreeably with the president, trustees, and faculty, can relieve the president of most financial responsibilities and worries and leave him free to deal with the important problems which are more within his experience and which constantly demand attention for the best service in the field of education.

For the proper and effective operation of the institution, it is essential that the business manager be under the president and that the president keep in close touch with the business operations. If full control passes to the business manager and if he is in final control of operations under the trustees, his tendency is to operate wholly for business results. The whole purpose of the expenditures is to facilitate education and research. Unless the president constantly keeps these objectives clearly before the business office and sees that first things toward the forwarding of the educational services are kept first, there is strong likelihood that business objectives will over-ride education.

In a very small college the business manager with one clerk may handle all this work. As the size of the financial operations increase, the staff will grow until in some of our large universities as many as 100 or more are employed.

The budget. No annual duty of the trustees is more important than the approval of the budget for the ensuing year. While it is true that the details of any large budget will probably be beyond the clear understanding of all or most of the trustees, these details can properly be left to the president and his advisers. There are, however, several very important things, the *most* important things about a budget, that are fully within the comprehension of every trustee.

Is the income conservatively estimated?

How do these estimates compare with the past year's experience?

Where there are variations from last year's receipts, on what are they based?

Does the budget balance? Are the expenses budgeted within the income? Are all anticipated expenses included in the budget?

Is there a reasonable reserve for unanticipated contingencies?

Budgets, like all other tabulations of figures, can be made to conceal the truth. The integrity of the budget presented by the president for approval should be checked carefully.

In any private institution dependent in part on annual gifts for current income, there is always a temptation to budget as much as it is *hoped* to receive. It would be sound business to budget only money already in hand from gifts at the beginning of the fiscal year, and hold all gifts received during the current year to be budgeted and used for the succeeding year. The pressure for current funds usually is too great to allow such a conservative policy.

The price a board of trustees pays in permitting the adoption of too liberal a budget is to tie the president to a money-raising program. A competent president can be of inestimable value in really directing the life and work of the college, but if his time and thought are absorbed in money-raising, he can do little else. A college, after all, is a long-time enterprise, and one in which a conservative policy will generally produce the finest results in the long run.

The preparation of the budget is carried out in various ways in different places. In a small institution it would be largely prepared by the president with such help as he required from the business manager and the dean. In a large institution the income is estimated in the financial office, and the recommendations for expenditures come up from the heads of departments, through the various deans to the president. The president in some cases turns over considerable responsibility for formulating the final budget to the financial officer and the deans, or to a committee; in other cases he himself gives much time and thought to the budget. It seems to the writer that the latter plan is sound. In the final analysis the preparation of the budget, doing the best possible justice to each salary demand and each departmental expense, is the most important matter that comes before the president each year.

The budget is the key to the administration of the institution; the operation of every detail is dependent on it. Its preparation gives opportunity for an annual survey of every single aspect of the institution. Inasmuch as the president is the only person equally interested in every part, and further, since he is responsible to the trustees for every department and enterprise, he would seem to be the only person qualified to prepare the budget.

The form of the budget is very important. Even a budget involving several million dollars expenditure can be so set up as to be within the understanding of most men. The usually accepted form opens with a one-page summary of income and a one-page summary of expenditures by colleges. There then follow the budgets of each administrative division. Under each is a one-page summary giving total expenditures for the division or department. This page is followed by final detailed budgets of each department in the college with each individual salary and other expenses. While no trustee could hope to judge the wisdom of each salary and item, he can grasp the distribution among the different colleges, the general salary range, and the relation of expense to income. The trustee must trust the president, deans, and other administrative offices for the wisdom and justice of details.

The trustees are responsible for the budget as finally approved. They are responsible to the legislature or donors, to the parents, and to the people at large, to see that the money is wisely and economically spent to promote the best service of the institution. They are under no direct pressure from deans and professors as the president must be. Each trustee should feel a keen responsibility to understand the budget and satisfy himself that it is conservative, includes all probable expenses, and is wise and just.

CHAPTER 5

THE PRESIDENT AND HIS APPOINTMENT

NO TASK that confronts a board of trustees is more difficult than the selection of a new president. The purpose of this chapter is to propose a method which will remove the uncertainty with which every board approaches the task and to make the undertaking a systematic one which can be approached with confidence.

The old adage that a stream cannot rise higher than its source certainly applies to a college and its president. No college can rise above the level of its president in maintaining standards, in enthusiasm for generous service, or in vision of opportunity. When the trustees choose a man to represent them in the administration of their institution, they are determining the level of excellence at which the institution will operate during his term of service. A president is either a leader and a stimulus to every person on the staff, or he is a check to ambition, a damper on enthusiasm, and spreads indifference or hopelessness through the ranks. This sounds exaggerated, but anyone who has served under able and under unqualified executives will recognize its truth. If it were possible to insure first-class leadership in the president's office of each of our 1,850 institutions, this would do more than any other one thing to improve American education.

When a board is satisfied with the services of an executive, it is always reluctant to change, and there is a strong tendency to retain the incumbent too long. It is rare that a president over 65 maintains the personnel and efficiency of his college at a high level. It would be best if 65 were fixed definitely as the retirement age for the president, as well as for all other administrative officers. In this case the board would know in advance exactly when this problem was to be faced.

Probably the happiest results are obtained by having a joint committee of the trustees and the faculty nominate candidates for President to the board. This seems wise for two reasons. The faculty will deeply appreciate the privilege of collaborating with the trustees in the search for the right man. Also, faculty members have to be consulted anyway in almost every case, and this can be done most easily, and with the least chance of the betrayal of confidence, if the faculty members consulted are formal members of the committee. Faculty members will appreciate this privilege of being represented on such a joint committee especially if they are requested to elect the members who will represent them. It is to be remembered that faculty members often have access to valuable information about men who are being considered that is not easily available to trustees. Sometimes the best plan seems to be for the trustees to request the faculty to elect a committee of five of their members with whom the trustees may confer and who may volunteer such aid as they can give.

All search should be largely limited in the first place to men between 35 and 52 years of age. There will be a few younger and an occasional man slightly older, but this age limit bars very few who are desirable and greatly simplifies the quest. A recent survey of 300 college presidents showed that very few over 52 years of age are appointed.

Next, determine as closely as possible what kind of man is wanted. This is best done by drawing up definite specifications. No man will qualify under all of them, but if *essential* qualifications are agreed upon, the search will be further simplified. The following outline will give an idea of the scope such specifications may cover. All points regarded as unimportant or on which there is not agreement should be omitted.

Age. What age limitation is desirable?

Family. Is it essential that he be a married man? That he have children?

Church. What is regarded as essential in his church relations?

Education. Is it desirable that his undergraduate work was done in any particular type of institution? What graduate degrees are required or preferred?

Scholarly Achievements. What, if any, publication or research work is required?

Educational Experience. What type and extent of educational experience is desired? What administrative experience is desirable?

Financial Experience. What experience in educational finance is essential?

Ability as Speaker. Is he required to be an able speaker? How high is this requirement rated?

Ability to Pick Men. Is it essential that he has proved his ability to select men wisely?

Ability to Raise Money. Is it essential that he be a man who has proved his ability to raise money?

Ability to Unify Faculty. Is it essential that he be a man who will unify the faculty and lead them to work together?

Ability to Deal With Students. Is it essential that he deal effectively with students and be liked by them?

This list is long, and probably much can be omitted in any one instance, but in it there must be some essential qualifications which will be necessary. To know them in advance is a great help, as it enables a committee to eliminate many names.

Where can trustees look for a president? Practically all college presidents are found in one or another of the following groups.

a. Members of the staff of the institution

b. Alumni of the institution

c. Successful presidents of other institutions

d. Deans in other institutions

e. Professors of administrative ability in other institutions

f. Men outside the teaching profession: clergymen, lawyers, businessmen, etc.

a. Always the first place to look is among the members of the staff between the ages of 35 and 52 years who stand high in the esteem of the faculty. Such a man knows the institution and its problems; he knows the members of the staff; his own weaknesses and strength are well known. The ablest presidents make serious effort to have men on their staffs capable of serving as presidents. In a university the Dean of the Graduate School should be worth consideration.

It is interesting to note that trustees are prone to consider men on the staff of their own institution from a different angle than that at which they look at other men. Of the men under consideration on their own college staff, they ask what disqualifying faults he has. Of the man from outside, they ask what his strong points are. This is a very unfair and short-sighted way to compare such men. An able and desirable man often is passed over in this way in favor of a man distinctly inferior to him. Many difficulties are avoided by appointing a man well known to the trustees and the staff, who is thoroughly acquainted with the institution in all its parts.

b. Along with a search of the staff, it is most desirable to search the alumni list among those aged 35 to 52 for anyone whose personality and experience recommends him highly for the appointment. His loyalty and earnest desire to serve usefully can be relied upon.

c. Where neither the staff nor the alumni offers a man on whom the trustees can agree, the search becomes far more difficult. The following procedure is offered as affording a

definite plan to include all possibly desirable individuals
in the country. It would seem worth consideration by most
of the 820 institutions listed in the 1948 edition of American
Universities and Colleges.

The present deans and presidents of our better known
institutions are all listed in *Who's Who in America*. It is not a
very difficult task for a competent secretary to check the
name of every dean and president born not more than 52
years ago. Such a survey made in 1954 would include all
born in 1900 or later.

After these names are checked, each biographical sketch
can be cut out, sorted into the year of birth and pasted alpha-
betically on cards 8½ x 11 inches. Such a study was made
of *Who's Who* for 1944–45, and about 500 names were listed.

If two or three men, who know the college or university
seeking a president and who are familiar with the colleges of
the country, will check carefully through this list, they usually
will find 30 to 50 men who might consider the vacant post and
who might be worth considering for the post. Of the entire
list, some are so situated that on account of the salary available or the distinction of their present appointment, they
would not consider the position. Many others, judged by the
post they hold or facts disclosed by the biographical sketch,
would not prove interesting candidates for the vacant position.
Between these two groups probably not more than 10 per
cent, and likely fewer, of the men on the list would seem
worth considering.

If the names on this smaller list are considered in the light
of the specifications agreed on for the president and discussed with a few people conversant with higher education,
as for example the executive director of the American College
Association, or the president of the American Council on
Education, the list usually can be cut down to about ten
men worthy of serious consideration. This final list would

have the *great value* that it would be *known* to contain the names of *nearly every person* worthy of further consideration.

From these ten names, it would be rather simple for the trustees, with such aid from the faculty as they desired, to eliminate six or eight and finally to select the man who would be best fitted for their presidency.

If there was a reasonable demand on the part of trustees for such a list as described above, it could be prepared readily and kept strictly up to date by one or another of our national educational associations. Photostatic copies could be placed in the hands of any board for a small fee which would fully cover the cost and be far less than it would cost individual boards to prepare the list for themselves.

d, e. There is one other important source of college presidents, especially for the less notable institutions which can pay only a modest salary. This is among the professors with a taste for administrative work and the deans who are not listed in *Who's Who*. The difficulty here is to secure a list of the 500 to 1,000 such men among the 140,000 college teachers. If college trustees or college faculty members were concerned, such a list could be prepared and kept up to date. However, when the president of an institution is acceptable, no need for such a list is felt, and when a vacancy occurs, the need is so urgent that there is no time to compile it.

The obvious national agency to maintain such a list is the American Association of University Professors. That association has an office in Washington, D. C., with an able secretary, and it has numerous members in every state.

If the Association of University Professors felt the need, a central committee with committees in every state could be set up. A state committee could easily inquire of faculty men in every college in the state, requesting the name and biography of every professor *under 52 years of age* who is locally regarded as competent to serve as president of some type of college. The type of college could be designated by his associates. This list, revised by the state committee, could be combined with lists from the other states by the central committee and put in shape for reference. After the lists were once prepared, the annual revision would be relatively simple. With the age limits of under 52 years, it is probable that the final list would be made up of less than 1,000 names. This could well be broken up into two or three lists based on current salary. For example $7,500 and up, $5,000 to $7,500, and under $5,000. If these lists—in photostat form—were kept available by the Association, any faculty could obtain them for an adequate fee. The expense could be met, and every faculty in the country could place in the hands of its trustees, when needed, a list of men regarded as competent by their associates. This would give every faculty a point of contact with the trustees in the selection of the president, a relationship which every faculty covets.

In one or the other of these two lists, any board could feel confident that 95 per cent of all available men would be presented who had suitable experience. The board's task would consist of eliminating names from one or both lists, then interviewing only a few men. If after working over such lists, the board turned back to a man on its own staff, the final decision would be made with great confidence.

f. The above plan omits consideration of clergymen, but each denomination is familiar with its own leaders and is quite competent to proceed without aid where a clergyman is desired.

In general, men outside the teaching profession who would be considered would be among the alumni of the college. Such appointments are not generally as successful as those of men who have developed in the field of education. Notable exceptions to this are well known, but the fact remains that the great majority of successful presidents have spent their earlier years in educational work.

While it seems extremely important, especially in a large, complex institution to appoint as president a man familiar with all aspects of education, at times the Board centers on a lawyer, clergyman, or business executive who really is unfamiliar with the detail academic work and problems. Such a man, if left in sole control can easily involve the institution unwittingly in difficulties in academic matters or problems related to the faculty.

When the appointment of such a man seems wise it should carry with it the appointment of a Vice President in charge of Education, on a parity with a Vice President in charge of Business and Finance. Such an officer, if wisely selected by the president, can relieve him of much burden and contribute enormously to the well being of the institution. Further, if the trustees are relieved of the necessity of finding a president capable of handling finance and education, their problem is greatly simplified and their field of choice is much wider.

While of course it would not be wise to burden the budget of a small college with such administrative officers, there are probably between 50 and 100 institutions in the country which could well support them.

The president's salary. It is a good general rule that the president should be paid twice the salary of the highest paid professorial rank. To pay more rather overemphasizes the importance of his office and tends to create discontent in the faculty. To pay less usually will make it very difficult to fill the position satisfactorily. The salaries of American college and university presidents range all the way from $5,000 to $30,000. Most of our forty largest institutions pay from $12,000 to $20,000. The great majority of our better colleges pays from $5,000 to $10,000. It is highly important to remember that the salary available is a distinct limitation on securing a successful president from another institution, for such a man is usually receiving as much or more than you can pay. On the other hand, almost anyone on the staff can be secured, as invariably the salary available for the president is greater than the institution pays any professor or dean.

Usually it is more satisfactory to pay the president an adequate salary and give him an allowance for travel expense and stop there, than to give him an entertainment fund or incidental fund. Any such fund must either be accounted for in minute detail, which is difficult, or merged with his salary in meeting his various expenses, which is very poor accounting practice.

In the great majority of cases a president's house is provided by the institution, and usually heat, light, and water are included. Where this is a simple, inexpensive residence commensurate with his salary (not costing more than twice his salary), it is reasonable to expect the president to pay out of his salary for service. Where the president's house is a grander mansion and perhaps beyond the reach of his salary, it is reasonable for the institution to provide also all or part of the cost of service.

It generally avoids criticism to allow the president to own his own car rather than to provide him with one. The college can properly pay him a reasonable mileage of from 3 to 6 cents a mile for its use in travel for the institution.

The business affairs, as they touch the president, should be so meticulously handled as to avoid any possible criticism of his integrity.

The tenure of the president. While the president is often considered to hold a very permanent place, he is, in fact, much less permanent than a professor. Three factors contribute to this situation. Many men are not appointed before they are 50 years old and at best should not serve beyond 65. Their terms will vary if all goes well from ten to fifteen years. If a man is appointed at about 40 years of age and makes a real success, he is very likely to be called to a better position in another institution before he is 55. Thus his term usually will be from ten to fifteen years at most. Then we have the many men appointed to presidencies which they fail to fill in a satisfactory manner and who are properly relieved of office after from two to six years. In general, the average term of service of a college or university president is less than twelve years.

It is exceptionally rare that a board is warranted in retaining a president in service beyond 65 years in age. While usually he is as intelligent and his judgment is as good at 65 as at 50, his vigor and eagerness to hunt for trouble and straighten it out is always far less. Much would be gained by fixing the age of retirement of presidents definitely at 65. Case after case can be cited where an able and distinguished president has been retained in office to 70 or 75 years of age or older, and where the institution materially deteriorated during the latter years of his service. It is increasingly the practice to retire the presidents of business corporations at 65 years of age, and this is certainly a good business precedent to follow. Also if retirement is definitely fixed at 65 the trustees will feel free, a year or two before the time for retirement of the president, to begin a search for his successor.

CHAPTER 6

THE RESPONSIBILITY OF THE TRUSTEES
AS A COURT OF APPEAL

WHILE the trustees are seldom appealed to in this capacity, the fact remains that the trustees are the final court of appeal for student, faculty, or the general public when they feel some injustice is being done in regular administrative channels. These matters may rise from disciplinary cases or scholarship failures of students; from failure to receive promotions in salary or rank by members of the staff; or from some business firm which feels that it has been discriminated against in competition for business. When such matters are brought to the trustees, it is best to hear complaints fully and also hear the administrative officer or faculty member involved and try to work out a solution that will avoid the recurrence of such appeals. It is unfortunate when the trustees feel unable to sustain the actions of their administrative officers, but if an error has been made or a real injustice done, certainly the administration should unite with the trustees in correcting it. If the administration is carried on capably and sympathetically, very few such cases will come before the trustees.

SECTION III

The Responsibilities of Trustees in Determining Policies Under Which a College or University Is Administered

A Discussion of Features of Administration
Which Are Properly Controlled by
Trustee Policy

CHAPTER 7

BACKGROUND FOR CONSIDERING
PRESENT COLLEGE PROBLEMS

IN ADDITION to being custodian of all property, appointing the president, and serving as a court of appeals, the chief function of the trustees is to formulate the policies governing the institution under their control.

Usually their policies have gradually developed in an informal way. Many policies actively followed are not formally recorded. It would seem, however, that one of the most important duties of the trustees should be to formulate, record, and publish its policies. From time to time they also should modify policies, and should hold the president to administering the institution under their policies.

Too often you hear the remark that the function and work of the trustees is to rubber stamp the actions and recommendations of the president. This certainly should not be so. The chief function of the trustees would more nearly seem to be to formulate policies, find out how closely the president is carrying them out, and determine what policies if any should be modified.

To illustrate the types of policies that might well be considered for adoption by trustees, a considerable number will be discussed. It is not thought that any single board would formulate fixed policies on all the subjects treated here. Rather it is hoped that if any of these matters come before a board, the discussions following will give a basis for comparison with the policy under discussion for adoption. Before entering on the discussion of various aspects of the college calling for some policy, it is desirable to give some general information about higher education today.

For Success, All Must Cooperate

"When the Trustees, the President, the Faculty, the Students, and the Alumni are all united in cordial cooperation and good will, an institution forges forward and accomplishes much. Without such cooperation, and upset by distrust, a faculty can do only inferior work and an institution can accomplish little. Seek good will, confidence and cooperation first."—Personal advice of Dr. Andrew D. Hepburn in 1911 to the author.

Each Institution Has a Personality of Its Own

Each college or university has a personality of its own. In every institution of distinction, this personality is well developed, and to it is due much of its influence and educational power.

The personality and individual character of an institution is a precious thing, as a man's personality is precious and should not be violated. An executive, supported by his trustees, who ruthlessly changes an institution to bend it to conformity to his ideas generally does more harm than good. No institution is perfect. All should change and grow stronger and better, but change and growth should be gradual. A president's term of ten years is only 1/100 of 1,000 years, an institution's reasonable life. If he can leave the institution as good and strong as he found it, or just a little stronger and rendering slightly better service, he has done well.

Types of Institutions

In this country there is such confusion in names, and such various combinations of courses in our institutions that no simple classification can be satisfactory. We can make a rather satisfactory classification of the *types* of major courses offered by our higher institutions.

1. College courses—the four years in arts and sciences based on four years of secondary school.

2. Technological courses—the four years in engineering, agriculture, home economics, etc., based on four years of secondary school, and designed through the application of the sciences to prepare the student for certain specific technical positions.

3. Teacher training courses—teachers colleges and normal schools, based on four years of secondary school, and offering training in the arts and sciences and in practice teaching with the purpose of training teachers for the elementary and secondary schools. The normal schools offer two years only and grant no degrees. The teachers colleges offer four years and confer the bachelor's degree.

4. University courses—theology, law, medicine, and graduate work in arts, sciences, and technology, all based on four years of undergraduate college work.

While the above is simple enough it is often confusing to designate a particular institution as belonging under one or the other classification, because of the fact that many offer two or more of the above types of courses, and some colleges, founded in the early days of this country, are misnamed universities. Massachusetts Institute of Technology and California Institute of Technology, while certainly schools of technology of the higher order, also carry on graduate work in certain fields equal to any university in the country. Bryn Mawr College and Lawrence College, while in every sense excellent colleges, also conduct graduate work of excellent university type in a few fields. Some universities in name and in quality of graduate work maintain no schools of medicine, law, or divinity which are usually regarded as essential parts of a university, e.g., Brown University, Princeton University. Various state colleges carry on extensive graduate work of university type, e.g., Iowa State College, Pennsylvania State College. Finally, numerous institutions bearing the name of universities make no pretense to do university work. They pride themselves on their undergraduate college, as for example, Wesleyan University, Bucknell University, DePauw University.

Probable Future of Higher Education

As a background for the study of these various policies, some idea is needed as to the probable future of higher education. Amid all our present turmoil, with world war, economic uncertainty, and political confusion, no one can predict with confidence the future of education, but we can look into the past and see the direction to which present tendencies point.

The proportion of children and youth to adults changes with the birth rate. In 1932–33 it was low; in 1941–45 it was high. The high school and college enrollment is affected both by the birth rate, which changes, and by the various pressures which steadily tend to send a larger percentage of youth through high school and on to college. The power of the pressures to send children to high school is seen in the figures for enrollment in Table 3.

TABLE 3
HIGH SCHOOL ENROLLMENT

Year	Youth of Age 14–17	High School Enrollment	Percentage of Youth 14–17 Enrolled
1880	4,265,000	110,000	2.6
1890	5,355,000	203,000	3.7
1900	6,134,000	519,000	8.5
1910	7,215,000	915,000	12.7
1920	9,341,000	2,200,000	28.3
1930	9,565,000	4,399,000	47.1
1940	9,726,000	7,113,282	72.6
1948	8,303,000	6,305,000	76.0

In 1938 some states enrolled more than 90 per cent of youth of high school age in high school, and fourteen states enrolled more than 80 per cent. On the other hand fifteen states enrolled less than 60 per cent. The enrollment of high school age youth is steadily gaining and we can confidently look forward to continued large increases in high school enrollment for a good many years, even with a decreasing birth rate. The maximum high school enrollment appears to be between 90 per cent and 95 per cent of the number of all youth fourteen to seventeen years of age.

In a similar way the trend of college enrollment is still upward and is likely to continue in that direction for some time to come. High school enrollment is still growing. While a great many high school graduates who are unable to do creditable college work now enter college, a large number who are well prepared for college do not enter. Our people are becoming aware of these facts, and it is probable that the condition will be gradually corrected. The steady pressure of various social forces to increase college enrollment is shown by the figures in Table 4.

TABLE 4
COLLEGE ENROLLMENT

Year	Youth of College Age 18–21	College and University Enrollment	Percentage of Youth 18–21 Enrolled
1880........	4,253,000	45,000	1.06
1890........	5,151,000	123,135	2.39
1900........	5,930,000	237,592	4.01
1910........	7,335,000	355,212	4.84
1920........	7,343,000	597,880	8.14
1930........	8,899,000	1,100,737	12.37
1940........	9,563,000	1,494,203	15.6
1948...	8,567,000	2,616,262	30.5

Since the early 1940's the numbers enrolled in college have been confusing. The drop in enrollment during World War II was succeeded by the abnormal increase due both to returning veterans and to the government aid to veterans attending college. In the 1950's we face both a trend toward return to normal enrollment and at the same time a loss due to drafting of college-age men for military service. Excluding all these distracting factors it seems probable that about 27.5 per cent of youth of college age may attend college.

Trustees may assume with confidence that the numbers of competent students applying for admission to college the country over will be maintained and will increase. The future of any particular institution can be estimated confidently against a background of increasing nation-wide demand for education above the high school level. The college's development will be based on the type of education it offers, its natural clientele, and its financial resources, present and prospective.

It also appears that the increasing pressure for larger college enrollment will be noted especially in our most outstanding colleges and universities, in publicly supported institutions with low tuition, and in institutions in great population centers, especially municipal universities with low tuition. There also will be increasing pressure for admission to free publicly supported junior colleges in cities of 10,000 or more.

The growth of junior colleges has been remarkable. They will undoubtedly become more and more a familiar adjunct of city public school systems. They should become terminal colleges for increasing numbers through provision of various vocational courses. A great future lies before our junior colleges as is indicated by their rapid growth (Table 5).

This phenomenal development and growth of junior colleges in the past thirty years must give great satisfaction to their founders, to their boards of trustees, and to their executives. They certainly fill an important place in American education. Their growth should impress the trustees of colleges and universities with two further facts. (1) The junior colleges will continue to provide one or two years of college training for an increasing number of local students. Perhaps half of these would otherwise have attended a four-year college or a university. Thus the latter will continue to enroll

TABLE 5

JUNIOR COLLEGES

Year	Number Jr. Colleges	Enrollment
*1919–20	52	8,102
1923–24	132	20,559
1927–28	248	44,855
†1931–32	436	74,088
1935–36	522	107,807
1937–38	528	129,106
1939–40	575	197,710
1940–41	610	236,162
1942–43	624	314,349
1944–45	584	249,788
1946–47	648	294,475
1948–49	651	500,536
‡1950–51	634	562,786

*Years 1919–28—*Statistics of Higher Education*, 1937–38, p. 10.
†Years 1931–42—*School and Society*, March 1, 1941, p. 286.
‡Years 1950–51—*Junior College Journal*, Vol. XXI, p. 131.

smaller or very slightly growing classes in the first and second year. On the other hand, half or more of the enrollment of the junior colleges is made up of students who would never otherwise have been able to go to college. (2) A large number of all these junior college students after one, or more generally two years in the local college, will transfer to the sophomore or junior year of a four-year college or to a university, thus steadily swelling the upper classes of these institutions. There is every reason to expect that enrollment in the junior colleges will continue their rapid growth. It is also probable that they will increasingly attempt to offer strong vocational terminal courses, especially the larger junior colleges.

Table 6 shows the very large enrollment of adults, largely

TABLE 6

JUNIOR COLLEGE DISTRIBUTION OF STUDENTS 1950–51

Freshmen	183,117
Sophomores	102,871
Special	44,031
Adults	214,407

in evening classes. The free, local junior college seems to attract adults more than any other type of college. As these colleges are more and more widely opened over the country we will probably see more than a million adults enrolled.

It seems probable that some four-year institutions located in cities could form advantageous affiliations with their respective city school systems, becoming the official junior college of the system, while continuing their regular four-year courses. Coe College in Cedar Rapids, Iowa; Toledo University in Toledo, Ohio; and the University of Akron in Akron, Ohio, face such opportunities. Each of these cities is amply large to warrant a strong junior college as a part of the school system. Unless such a college is organized cooperatively between the local institution and the city schools it would seem likely to be organized sometime separately as a part of the school system.

A junior college supplementing the city schools, and offering terminal courses especially designed to train young men and women in two years for employment in local industry and business, can be of great value to the community, to the young people, and to business. The local junior college has a variety of functions, some quite different from those of an ordinary four-year college located in a city.

This background survey would not be complete without

TABLE 7

TEACHERS COLLEGES AND NORMAL SCHOOLS

Year	1909–10	1919–20	1929–30	1935–36	1937–38	1948–49
Enrollment Sept.–June.....	88,561	135,435	161,524	136,926	134,693	190,342
Non-degree Graduates.....	15,430	21,012	49,227	14,448	10,651	....
Graduates with Degree........	....	1,296	11,073	18,262	20,422	23,031
Graduate Students	....	....	....	664	1,020	4,922

some consideration of our teachers colleges and normal schools. The former offer one or more four-year courses leading to degrees. There were 260 institutions included in the Report of the United States Office of Education for 1947–48 (Table 7), beyond which are projected more recent figures.

It is evident that the separate teachers' training college, while growing, is not keeping pace with the junior college or with the 4-year liberal arts colleges. It also is clear that the 2-year normal school is generally losing out. While 31,000 teachers were graduated in 1949–50, this is far from enough to fill the vacancies in the teaching staffs of our elementary schools occurring annually. This need probably demands 100,000 to 150,000 teachers a year, if adequately met.

With confidence in the general future of college and university education and due consideration for the peculiar services offered and limitations controlling enrollment, each board should carefully consider the long-time future of the institution for which it is responsible.

Of all our American institutions the colleges and universities are perhaps the most permanent. While the churches as national organizations may be equally permanent, the individual centers of worship shift with population shifts. In Europe there are many universities which have been on their present sites for from 500 to 1,000 years. Each is more vigorous and full of life now than ever before. We may well look on most of our American colleges and universities as equally permanent. If we think of an institution as having a natural life of 1,000 years or more, the urgency for physical improvements becomes less, and the importance of able intellectual leaders for the present, seems more urgent. We are certainly concerned with the present; buildings will come. That leadership is best which points toward better education rather than toward better buildings.

The Importance to a Small College of Distinct Appeal
or Distinctive Personality

In the early days all colleges were small. The great majority of students came from the small area near the college. All colleges were much alike.

Today all this is changed. Distance is a minor obstacle to the student. Many institutions now receive more than 25 per cent of their students from outside the state in which they are located; 94 per cent of Dartmouth students come from outside New Hampshire. Colleges differ greatly among themselves in the courses offered, the clientele to which they appeal, and in the quality of students admitted.

The state universities have grown enormously, offer a wide variety of courses, and charge low tuition. They offer strong competition to the small colleges which have developed no individual strong appeal of their own.

On the other hand, our best colleges of high standards, and those which for some reason appeal strongly to some special group or type of patrons, have more applicants for admission than can be accepted. Sarah Lawrence College, Swarthmore, Oberlin, Antioch, Haverford, Vassar, California Institute of Technology, and a good many more, each year turn away hundreds of applicants for admission. Many other colleges have all they can accept each year. The private colleges enrolling 400 to 800 students can offer their students much that the great public institution with thousands of students cannot offer. When they try to imitate the state university in offering a wide range of subjects, they waste their opportunity. To succeed they must be strong in some aspect of service in which the great university with thousands of students cannot compete. The small college must be outstandingly strong in some aspect of service in which it can be outstandingly strong. Some of our best colleges maintain

high standards of admission and high scholarship requirements for continued residence. Some give the most careful
attention to fitting instruction to the needs of the individual
student. Some appeal strongly to the membership of certain
religious denominations. Some require every student to earn
part of his expenses and so give real experience in labor.
Almost without exception those colleges which really give a
valuable service to their students beyond the usual routine
course have all the students for which they can well care.
It is true, however, that the day is past or rapidly passing
when any college offering a usual arts course and with no
special advantage can count on a good enrollment of local
students.

CHAPTER 8

ENROLLMENT, ADMISSION REQUIREMENTS, AND LIMITATION OF NUMBERS

WITH the purpose of illustrating the types of problems which can properly be controlled by trustee policy, and also to give some information as to common practice about these aspects of college administration, a considerable number of problems, frequently before the president and trustees, will be discussed at some length. As we have 1,880 different sets of conditions limiting our 1,880 institutions, no two are exactly alike, and much that follows will not be applicable to any particular one. However, reference by a trustee to a subject discussed here will enable him to enter on consideration of the matter as it applies locally, with some useful background.

College Students, Enrollment Limitation, and Admission Requirements

A college must have students; the whole operation revolves about the students. Naturally, there is much concerning students in which the trustees should interest themselves. In the first place it is highly desirable for the trustees to determine the number of students which the institution should enroll.

Who Should Go to College

This is a question that is much debated. Each parent is usually sure that his child should go, but he is doubtful about some of his neighbors' children. One school of thought urges that it is the duty of the college to offer courses suitable to the needs and ability of every youth, that the college should suit its standards and requirements to the needs of youth. Another school urges that altogether too many are now going to college, that we are training far too many for white collar jobs and spoiling many laborers, tradesmen, and mechanics.

Combining the suggestions of the psychologists that about 10 per cent of all youth have the native ability to profit greatly by college training, with our experience at Iowa State College, it seems probable that about 12 per cent of youth would well repay the expense of four years of college training. Probably 15.5 per cent more would profit from one or two years in college, especially if ample opportunity were offered for vocational work. Nationally we now have about 14.6 per cent of youth of college age in college. Of these probably a quarter lack the ability or the ambition necessary to profit largely. On the other hand, there are a great many youth not in college who would profit greatly from college training. If we are able to exclude the least worthy and replace them with others with the ability and eagerness for college but now excluded by lack of money, we shall see the college enrollment increase somewhat further.

From the above we conclude that the present enrollment is not too large; in fact it probably should still increase. On the other hand, it would be advantageous to all if those unqualified to profit from college were excluded and replaced by an equal number of able youth who are not now financially able to attend.

Size of Enrollment

There is no greater fallacy than that constantly growing enrollment is desirable. Each institution at a given time has a certain optimum enrollment which it can serve best. This optimum is fixed by income, physical plant, types of work offered, and size of faculty. It may be greater or less than the actual current enrollment. Its determination is important, and when the trustees fix the enrollment to be aimed at, this

figure determines many others—the size of faculty, number
and size of class and laboratory buildings, dormitories needed,
and income required. As time passes, the demands for service
and the institutional resources change, and the trustees will
be obliged to resurvey the situation and perhaps change the
enrollment goal. However, they will serve their trust much
better by keeping the enrollment at a carefully determined
figure than by letting matters drift and hailing every increase
as a welcome gain.

The present enrollment in our 1,880 colleges and universities varies from less than 50 to over 40,000 in actual attendance at one time. It is evident that the matter of size has
many aspects. These can best be considered by taking the
different types of institutions separately.

In a *junior college*, covering two years of college work only,
we have one type of problem. Most junior colleges are public
institutions, administered as a part of the public school systems.
Many are housed in the high school buildings. In all public
junior colleges tuition should be free. The usual tuition is
$100 a year. For reasonable efficiency such colleges should
enroll as a minimum at least 100 students and preferably 200.
With such an enrollment and with $100 tuition, they can be
operated without great expense to the school system and with
value to the community. On the other hand, in many of our
large cities we have junior colleges enrolling several thousand
students, and generously equipped with buildings. In every
case the size will depend on the financial resources, the variety of courses offered, and the number of high school graduates living within convenient distance. The most common
error is to open a junior college in a community too small
either to provide a minimum number of students, or to finance
the enterprise.

Privately supported junior colleges usually limit their enrollment to numbers determined by endowment, fees charged,
and the type of service they plan to render.

Another problem is presented by the *four-year colleges*. The great majority of these are liberal arts colleges with enrollments from 400 to 2,000. While in some cases the tuition charged is as high as $600, it is usually from $150 to $300. Maximum salaries usually range from $2,500 to $5,000 or $7,500. Endowment income varies greatly. It is easy to see that within this group, widely varying conditions exist. In general it is most economical, and most efficient in other ways, to enroll at least 400 students. As educational practice now stands, a certain minimum number of different departments must be maintained in a college. Four hundred students permit this minimum number of departments, with adequate staff and reasonably sized classes. Up to 400, each additional student brings in tuition with no increase in expense. Above 400 the additional expense for added instructors, etc., is likely to be greater than the tuition received. An increase above 400 should be determined largely by the endowment income. The total cost per student must be met by the net income from tuition per student plus the net income from endowment per student.

Some institutions maintain an enrollment that appears to be much below their financial resources because there the desirable number is fixed for some special purpose. Haverford College, which has always maintained very high requirements for admission, has a small enrollment. Sarah Lawrence College is endeavoring to adapt its educational services very exactly to the needs of each individual student. This program cannot be carried out with large numbers.

Each institution justifies careful study. Size without quality is a poor basis for operation. It is far better to limit size and maintain creditable standards of admission and reasonable salaries for the staff.

It is also worthy of remark that in areas where other similar institutions are near at hand, a limited enrollment is more reasonable than in areas where no other institution is available.

Among the *universities* quite a different enrollment problem is faced. These institutions are made up of a number of separate colleges or schools and many major departments. Each college and department presents an enrollment problem. It is essential that a certain minimum number, different in each case, be enrolled for reasonable efficiency. Also many schools and departments have maximum enrollment limits fixed by factors beyond control; for example, clinical and hospital facilities put a definite limit on the enrollment in a medical school. However, there are always numerous departments and colleges for which the enrollment must be determined by the trustees or left indeterminate. The tendency of any college in a university or any department left to itself is to increase its enrollment as much as possible and thereby magnify its importance in the institution.

In institutions laying stress on the graduate college, it is essential that the staff be adequate to carry both graduate and undergraduate work. This often raises a serious question whether undergraduate enrollment will be limited to allow for the development of the graduate college, or whether graduate work will be put in second place and undergraduate enrollment remain unlimited. This problem is now confronting all our larger state universities. The importance of graduate and research work carried by them is certainly increasing.

Privately-supported universities usually have limited their enrollments, while publicly-supported universities have not done so—except in certain fields such as medicine. Tables 8 and 9 show the magnitude of eight among our leading institutions for which data is available on enrollment and budgets. As shown, the enrollment is materially larger in the public institutions cited than in the private schools.

The total expenditures given cover many different entries. At the Massachusetts Institute of Technology, 58 per cent of the expenditures given are for contract research.

TABLE 8
PRIVATE UNIVERSITIES

Year	School	Enrollment	Total Budget
1948–49....	University of Chicago	13,271	$38,978,991
1946–47....	Columbia University	20,947	14,546,321
1948–49....	Harvard University	11,704	20,729,534
1948–49....	Massachusetts Institute of Technology	5,433	23,353,000

In the private institutions listed in Table 8, where only selected students are admitted and the number admitted each year is limited, high tuition fees of $700 to $800 are charged. The income is largely from endowments and student fees. Large numbers of generous scholarships are awarded to able students.

In the public institutions there is much less emphasis on admitting only well prepared students. Since these institutions are state supported in large part, funds can be obtained to care for heavier enrollments. Tuition is low—from $60 to $200 to students from within the state boundaries.

TABLE 9
PUBLIC UNIVERSITIES

Year	School	Enrollment	Total Budget
1949–50....	University of Illinois	23,873	$49,341,974
1949–50....	University of Michigan	19,893	18,662,757
1949–50....	University of Minnesota	24,121	24,339,625
1949–50....	University of Wisconsin	20,865	27,976,301

The private institutions graduate a large percentage of those admitted. The public institutions graduate a much smaller percentage, because many of those admitted are unable to do the work creditably. There is a strong growing sentiment across the nation that ample, free, publicly-supported junior colleges, trade and technical schools—above high school—should be provided. In this case the public universities (as is practiced in California) would admit anly students who have shown the ability to do the work required. Such a limitation would result in better service to all students, better economy of operation, and in higher standards in the institutions.

In all universities, public and private, the question of optimum size is of serious concern to the trustees. These great and important institutions, costly and serving a wide variety of interests, should be studied constantly to determine what departments or colleges are too large or too small, what should be added and what should be discontinued, what are most expensive, and whether they warrant their cost. It is only as the president and trustees consider the results of such studies that they can wisely guide these institutions to their most valuable services to society.

Admission Requirements

Formerly, great stress was placed on the subjects an entering student had studied. This emphasis is still marked, but there is general recognition of the fact that the subjects studied are less significant than the quality of the student's mind and his interest and ability to apply himself to study. A student ranking in the upper one-fifth of his class in the secondary school has a very high probability of success in college, while students in the lowest third of their secondary school class can have little hope of graduation from college regardless of what they studied.

Of our 1,880 universities, colleges, teachers colleges, and

junior colleges, by far the greater number accept any student who applies for entrance, provided he has been graduated by an accredited high school.

This results in the admission of a very large number who lack the preparation and the motivation to do creditable work in college and to graduate. Depending on the type of institution and its standards, from 30 to 60 per cent of those admitted on high school certificates without any further requirement fail to graduate.

While at first thought this might seem a reflection on the high schools, it is really not so. The high schools are open to all who finish the grades, offer all types of work, and make no pretense that all their graduates are prepared to do college work. If the high school principal is asked seriously to recommend students for college entrance, he rarely recommends those who are graduated in the lower half or third of their class. The high school emancipated itself from the status of a college preparatory school several decades ago and prides itself on being the terminal school for many pupils, and to that end usually offers many courses which make no pretense of being preparatory to college.

The free admission of all high school graduates, where practiced, is based on one of the following reasons:

1. The institution seeks numbers regardless of quality.
2. The college is a democratic institution and therefore should be open to all.
3. Any taxpayer's child who is a high school graduate is entitled to enter a publicly supported institution.

None of these reasons is sound. Every college, however elementary, has standards, and when students are admitted who cannot and will not meet these standards and are forced to drop out, both the college and the student suffer.

In most cases publicly supported institutions hesitate to fix high admission requirements or to put a limit on enrollment. All students who are graduates of standard high schools are accepted in the freshman year on their certificates. Of course, the great majority of all those who rank in the lower half of their high school classes fail to graduate, and many fall out during the first year. Everyone knows that college is more difficult than high school; that the majority of those entering college were graduated from the upper one-third of their high school classes; and that students whose interest in learning is so slight that they are content to remain near the bottom of their high school classes for four years are extremely unlikely to do creditable work in college in competition with much more capable students. With all this common knowledge, it seems strange that this policy of admitting all high school graduates is continued. It is doubtful whether students graduating in the lowest third of their high school classes get any considerable benefit in college. It is surely doubtful wisdom to admit students to courses in which there is no chance of success. A much wiser plan would be to admit on certificate students graduating in the upper one-fourth or upper one-third of their classes and require those of lower rank to prove their ability to do college work by passing a reasonable entrance examination.

Not only is the admission of unprepared and weakly motivated students of very slight value to them, but it is a useless expense to the state or municipality, and it tends strongly to lower the general level of standards in the institution. It is probable that changes for the better will come about in this matter before many years pass. The theory that the state or the city will provide adequate funds to suitably instruct all who enter is less and less true.

Even now our publicly supported penitentiaries, insane hospitals, institutions for the feeble minded, and hospitals for treatment of tuberculosis, all have very strict requirements for admission, and state universities for quite different but equally important reasons should follow their example.

Of our 1,880 institutions about 30 have very high require-

ments for admission—graduation from an accredited school
in the highest one-seventh or one-fifth of the class or by passing the college entrance board examination. Of these institutions a number admit from those thus qualifying only a
limited number who through a personal interview by a staff
official seem most promising. As most of these institutions
strictly limit the number of freshmen and as they have two
or three times as many qualified applicants for admission,
such requirements are wise and very reasonable.

Between these two extreme groups a few hundred institutions require something more than mere graduation from high
school.

As has been remarked in other connections, far too many
American colleges and universities pride themselves on numbers to their serious disadvantage. At least moderate entrance
requirements beyond mere graduation from high school, such
as limiting admission on certificate to those in the upper half
of the class, would be reasonable and would exclude those
who could profit least. It would tend to raise standards and
reduce costs, and would relieve administrative officers, parents,
and students of many unhappy hours. The time must surely
come when there is better vocational guidance and better
cooperation between secondary schools and colleges to the
end that students in the secondary schools who lack qualifications for college work will become fully aware while in the
secondary school that college has nothing to offer them. At
the same time our country needs widely distributed vocational
training schools, accepting students at high school graduation
or possibly after two years in high school, and giving them
training for specific employment, somewhat below the level
of college graduates and in lines which require youth with
some special training for useful employment. The free junior
colleges may develop so they will meet this demand. However, at present the typical junior college merely duplicates
the first two years of a liberal arts college.

It is certainly a very important duty of trustees to maintain a carefully defined policy relative to admissions, such as will best conserve the standards of their institution and give the best service to their constituents. This will usually involve (1) a determination of the number of entrants that the institution can most advantageously accept and (2) fixing entrance requirements that will secure the most competent among the applicants to fill that number.

The Limitation of Enrollment

Many institutions have a definite numerical limit to the number that may be admitted to the first-year class, either in the whole institution or in one or more departments. Such a fixed limit usually operates so that only the best prepared applicants are admitted.

As standard requirements for medical school instruction now stand, the first-year class in every good medical school is definitely limited to the number who can be well accommodated with clinic and hospital facilities. Admission to each of the seventeen veterinary colleges in the country is limited similarly. Admission to other university colleges could well be limited to a number who could be placed in professional positions on graduation.

Limitation of enrollment in the graduate school of every institution could well be imposed. This applies especially to those entering on the work for the doctorate. While admission to study for the master's degree should be reasonably liberal, there seems to be little reason to admit any but very able students to study for the doctorate, where high scholarship and real competency in research are supposed to be required. The fact that 138 institutions conferred the doctorate in 1948–49 on 5,293 persons would seem to indicate that in many cases high ability was not required. Each institution could well redefine its purpose in maintaining a graduate school; re-evaluate its degrees and the fields in which they are conferred; and consider the demand for graduates with advanced degrees, and the institutions offering graduate work similar to that which it offers. In the light of such a study an institution could determine what limitations on graduate work would be wise for itself.

The trustees of every institution should concern themselves with problems of enrollment, not just inquire as to whether the total enrollment has increased—such inquiries are very common—but insist on constant studies of the desirable enrollment in each college, school, and department with a view to determining what specific enrollment, under existing conditions, will yield the best results for the students, for the institution, and for service to the public.

CHAPTER 9

THE CAMPUS AND BUILDINGS

WHEN the trustees have determined the desirable number of students to be enrolled, they are in a position to estimate their needs for land. An educational institution rarely has too much land for campus and recreation.

Sports and athletics for all students are more and more generally recognized as highly desirable. Well-kept playing fields near the living quarters of the students are great incentives to exercise. As soon as a campus is surrounded by business or residential buildings additional land may easily cost $10,000 to $30,000 an acre. Including golf and all out-door sports, a fairly generous area for sports and athletics would require an acre of well-developed sports area for every twenty to fifty students. Unless it were endowed or financed in some special way, a college golf course would not be practical for a small college. For campus proper probably an acre for fifty students would allow generous space; of course, in a city where land sells by the square foot rather than by the acre, much less is ample.

A study by an able landscape architect of the site and buildings together with the location of anticipated future buildings, athletic field, and play grounds, will quickly reveal the land needs. Every effort should be made to provide for these.

Usually any landscape plan has to be modified as time goes on. Changes in size, objectives, alteration in building plans, etc.—all tend to change the campus plans. A revision of the plans from time to time to meet these needs will retain the symmetry of the campus and allow for changing demands.

An annual item in the budget for trees and shrubs will mean

a very great deal for beauty and will provide for trees that die or must be removed on account of improvements.

The services of a landscape architect are indispensable in the wise, intelligent, and beautiful development of any campus.

The trustees' responsibility is to see that a competent landscape architect is employed, to see that it is arranged for him to work with the president and the college architect in developing and modifying plans, and to approve or disapprove final plans and changes.

Building Plans

As occasion arises to erect new buildings, the responsibilities of the trustees are to select or approve the selection of an architect, to study and approve the type of architecture proposed, and finally to approve the building plans.

The board will ordinarily have a building committee which will have legal authority to act for the board on detail, approve estimates of contractors, etc. The board as a whole would approve the architect, determine with his advice the type of architecture, approve the plans for a specific building, and approve its location.

One of the common errors in college buildings is to erect buildings so designed that they cannot well be enlarged. Unless the total enrollment is definitely fixed, it often becomes necessary to enlarge buildings. If the chemistry building is too small, either it must be enlarged or a new building must be built. Wherever possible some provision for enlargement should be included in the plans.

It cannot be too strongly emphasized that the department which is to use a building should be fully consulted by the architect, and that the preliminary plans should have the approval of the department before being adopted. Unless this is insisted on, the architect will often hurry the plans to completion, and the resulting building will be much less serviceable than it otherwise could be.

Not only should there be a campus plan worked out by a competent landscape architect in collaboration with the administration until acceptable to the trustees, but building plans should be prepared in advance of needs, or at least in advance of funds for building, that will harmonize with present buildings and that will allow generously for future growth.

Often when money becomes available, either through a gift or through state appropriations, there is pressure to build quickly, and the preparation and consideration of plans are unduly hastened. College and university buildings, while conforming to certain types, differ greatly in detailed use. Much the best results are obtained if the architect can work at leisure, cooperating with the department involved, in working out floor plans, space needs, plans for the enlargement of the building if such will probably be needed, and the development of a sketch plan of the exterior. If such preliminary plans can be developed in advance of procuring the funds necessary for building, to the point of obtaining the approval of the department, the president, and the trustees, the ultimate satisfaction in the building is largely assured. A competent architect and landscape architect, both sympathetic with the institution and willing to cooperate fully with each other and with the president and department heads to produce what will be most serviceable, and a board of trustees demanding that building needs be largely anticipated, will save many regrets and much waste. A book by C. Z. Klauder on *College Architecture*, and a number of booklets on college buildings, published by the American College Association, may be found of value to trustees of colleges. They aim to cover the needs of colleges rather than those of the great universities.

CHAPTER 10

THE SCOPE OF THE WORK OF AN INSTITUTION

ONE of the most important policies of any educational institution is to determine its scope. This policy should always be carefully and definitely fixed by the trustees and modified by them as circumstances warrant.

The executive is constantly under pressure and temptation to expand and broaden the scope of instruction. Yielding too readily to such pressure involves the institution in increased expenditures and often in unwise duplication of work elsewhere.

The problem is quite different in the college and in the university.

The College

In a small college probably the smallest possible number of separate departments would be six:

Ancient and modern languages
English language and literature
Social sciences (history, economics, and sociology)
Mathematics and physical sciences (physics and chemistry)
Biological sciences (zoology and botany)
Philosophy, psychology, and education

Here six professors with such assistant professors and instructors as needed could carry the work of a small liberal arts college. Six professors and eight or nine instructors could teach adequately 200–250 students.

As finances and enrollment justified, this could gradually be expanded to eighteen or twenty or more departments, each with a full professor in charge with such associate and assistant professors and instructors as are needed and can be properly financed. Such an organization might well include the following departments:

English language and literature
Modern languages (Spanish, German, and French)
Ancient languages (Latin and Greek)
History
Economics and sociology
Psychology
Education
Philosophy and religious education
Mathematics
Physics
Chemistry
Biology (botany, zoology, and geology)
Music
Art
Physical education for men
Physical education for women

The expansion should certainly be cautious, care being taken that the existing departments are strong before any additions are made. Departments should be added in the order in which they will serve the largest number, and most truly serve the students.

It is more desirable to have able teachers than many teachers. While in many small colleges with ample funds, a ratio of one teacher to ten students is maintained, and even as low as one to seven has been observed, still excellent work can be done with a ratio of one teacher to fifteen students, and even with one teacher to twenty students. In most cases, with relatively inadequate funds, better general results will be obtained with higher salaries and abler teachers, rather than with more, less able teachers on low salaries. The total available for salaries is always rather closely fixed, and the average salary must always be determined by the number of teachers.

Most small colleges are very sensitive to the competition for students with large state universities with low fees and a rich variety of courses. They are constantly tempted to enrich their curriculum by adding courses and instructors. No college can compete with a large institution in the variety of courses offered. The chief strength of the college must lie in the intimacy of smaller numbers, in the personal acquaintance of faculty and students, in special services to the individual not possible with great numbers, and in such special emphasis as each college may stress, as for example, serving the young people of a particular religious denomination, as at Ohio Wesleyan, or in offering honors courses to very able students, as at Swarthmore.

The whole financial problem of any college largely revolves about the ratio of students to teacher and the number of separate departments maintained. The trustees should be concerned that a sound policy along these lines is fixed for their college.

The University

Under the designation "universities," we are including all institutions encouraging research on a considerable scale and offering graduate work for the doctorate. There are between 75 and 125 institutions more or less properly included here. Their problem is much more complicated than that of the college.

With a few exceptions their work is organized into a group of colleges, so the first question of policy relates to what colleges or schools the institution should maintain. Usually every one of these institutions will have a college of liberal arts, or a college of science, or both. Almost without exception there will also be a graduate school or graduate college. In addition there may be from one or two to ten or more colleges each with a dean and separate faculty. The more usual are law, medicine, theology, dentistry, engineering, education, journalism, business and commerce, agriculture, veterinary medicine, home economics, fine arts. Various other schools and colleges may be found in our universities. The wisdom of including all or any of these colleges in a given university system is an important matter for the trustees to decide. A creditable medical school enrolling 250 or more students must have access to a large and well-run hospital. The annual budget will be well over $500,000 and may be $1,000,000 or $1,500,000. The country needs a certain number of medical school graduates each year. In 1950 there were 70 accredited four-year medical colleges in the United States. Nine four-year medical colleges are located in Canada. The question of whether to add a medical school and if so how large, with what special lines of research and financed by how large a budget—all are matters of policy vital to the trustees, and the enterprise should not be undertaken unless they are assured that such a school is badly needed, and that they have ample funds to carry it on successfully.

Every university will need to maintain a college of arts and science, to provide basic work, not only leading to a bachelor's degree but giving courses essential to all the other colleges. The desirability of each additional college should be determined on the basis of need and finance. Some of our smaller state universities neither need nor can adequately finance many colleges. Some colleges, as for example, medicine, can well be left to larger, nearby institutions. Other fields, such as journalism, may be provided for by a few courses in the arts and science college rather than by offering more extensive courses organized in a college of journalism.

Further, some fields of training employ a rather limited number of trained men, and these can be prepared in a small number of institutions; for example, seventeen veterinary colleges supply the forty-eight states with veterinarians.

The same type of questions arise relative to each department authorized in each college. Shall a college of engineering offer civil, mechanical, and electrical engineering only, or shall departments of chemical, mining, structural, sanitary, nautical, aeronautical engineering, etc., be added. In each case the first question relates to the real need for the department, and whether, if it is provided, enough students will enroll to justify the employment of an adequate number of capable instructors; whether the demand for trained men in the field is already adequately supplied by existing departments; and whether, if graduates are turned out, they can be placed in suitable positions. Finally, will the budget stand the added expense?

Another question should always be considered. To what extent is it planned to carry on research and graduate work in the proposed department? This is an important question, for significant research and graduate work leading to the doctorate certainly cost money.

The consideration of research and graduate work can very properly be considered in three grades.

Almost any department with competent instructors can and should carry on minor, inexpensive research for the satisfaction and growth of its staff members. Such a department can properly offer work for the masters degree occasionally without appreciable added expense. Such minor research and graduate work might almost always be approved.

If, however, it is proposed to employ professors of recognized research ability and provide them with adequate research facilities, and train students for the doctorate, very considerable expense is involved and should be anticipated.

Research and graduate work can be carried on at a still

higher level where the institution seriously endeavors to maintain a department in the very first rank. In each highly specialized field of knowledge, as for example, in plant physiology, atomic physics, municipal government, or labor problems, there are only a very few, perhaps three to ten outstanding men in America, and they command salaries of from $7,500 to $15,000. If an institution proposes to rank at the top in any field, it must maintain on its staff one or more of the ablest men in the field. Any notable institution may properly be ambitious to maintain a few distinguished research departments, but only the very richest can maintain more than a few. Six of our strongest graduate schools each offer graduate work for the doctorate in only about 60 per cent of the fifty-one fields listed in "Doctoral Dissertations" and are doing outstanding work in less than half this number. Many of these fifty-one fields could well be subdivided into from two to ten important subfields.

Most institutions entitled to be classed broadly as universities may be offering work in from 50 to 100 departments. It is certainly the business of the trustees to determine in which of the following categories each of these departments is maintained:

a. Strictly a service department, offering undergraduate courses, but no graduate work whatever and carrying on no specially financed research.

b. Largely a service department for undergraduate work, but offering work for the masters degree and doing minor research.

c. Offering undergraduate and graduate courses and training students for the doctorate. Carrying on extensive research work.

d. Maintaining graduate and research work ranking with the best in America and staffed with one or more of the most distinguished men in the field.

Too often, in the absence of rigid control by trustees and president, all departments attempt to offer graduate work for the doctorate, and much mediocre work is done. Particularly for the doctorate, distinction comes only from graduating able men who fully maintain the reputation of the institution. It is far better and more useful to maintain truly high grade graduate and research work in a limited number of departments peculiarly suited to the type of institution and its location, than to spread out into more fields than can be financed at a high level.

The trustees are too prone to accept the organization of an institution as it is without question. They overlook the fact that every institution has grown through opportunity, through the enthusiasms of donors, presidents, and trustees; that during weak administrations strong professors have pushed their departments to an unwarranted prominence; and that some departments are weak that should be strong. They also sometimes forget that a college or university is a living, changing organism, maintained to serve a changing society. It is also very conservative and responds to pressures slowly. Every department and college should be constantly scrutinized in the light of current social needs, and the trustees should assure themselves that in each field, support is in proportion to the demand for service. Departments and colleges which cease to be necessary should be discontinued. New departments and colleges for which there is a real need should be established.

Public Relations

Years ago our colleges and universities were largely limited to the campus in the scope of their influence. They did no appreciable research for the public. Their curricula were largely general and few students were trained for specific jobs. Little or no extension work was carried on.

Today this is changed. The influence of the larger institutions is widespread. The public sentiment for or against institutions of higher education is definitely important to them. Relations with the public has grown to be a matter of large concern to every college and university in the land.

This is discussed ably by Professor Scott M. Cutlip.* Quoting him in part: "In simple terms public relations embody any situation, act, or word which influences people—favorably or unfavorably. The public relations of a college, then, are made up of all the impressions it creates—good or bad. These impressions are made by an institution's policies, its performance, its people, and its publicity. The last is the least important. The nub of sound public relations is good performance that is understood and appreciated. Public relations—as a technique—embodies the ways and means of achieving good performance that is understood and appreciated."

Since public relations are so important, they should be a matter of careful consideration by the Trustees. Whether a separate official should be employed as director of public relations will depend upon the size of the institution and upon the skill of the president in this field. It is important for the Trustees to be well informed on the standing of their institution in the public mind. Their public includes the students in college, the faculty, the college world, and the general public. Depending upon whether the institution is public or private, the standing with the State Legislature or with men of affairs who might be interested in helping sustain the institution financially also ranks as an important consideration.

Certainly the first factor on which good public relations will depend is the quality of the teaching, and the care of and welfare of the students. In a university the reputation for

---

* American Association of University Professors *Bulletin*, Vol. 36, pp. 646 *et seq.*

able research is highly important. The financial integrity of the institution in all relations and in every detail is vital. The reputations of the president, deans, and directors for frankness, truthfulness, and integrity is essential. Publicity of value is based on these factors.

Many institutions now employ a man in charge of a department of public relations. In some cases he is a vice president. He should certainly try to see not only that the publicity given out is fully supported by the quality of the work done and the character of the staff, but also he should be conscious of the weaknesses of the institution. As far as possible he then should endeavor to see that these weaknesses are *corrected*. A public relations man cannot cover up or make up for the weaknesses of an institution.

CHAPTER 11

THE FACULTY

MANY of the problems confronting the trustees relate to the faculty. A happy, contented faculty, working efficiently and in cordial cooperation with each other and with the administration, depends largely on the policies affecting them and their work that are adopted by the trustees and followed by the administration.

The trustees should never lose sight of the fact that nothing can take the place of inspiring teachers of fine personality and noble character.

All teachers impart knowledge to their students; some few leave a personal imprint of their character and personality on their students. These latter are the men and women who really teach and develop the best that is in the students. These teachers are personally acquainted with their students; they do most for small classes, through intimate contact. They open themselves to their students and give them freely of their experience and wisdom as well as of their knowledge. Such teachers are never forgotten. The memory of them and their classes remains a permanent part of the student long after all knowledge acquired there has been forgotten or merged in one's general body of information. Fortunate are the students who come under such teachers. Fortunate are the institutions, which in these days of specialization and detailed research, number such teachers on their faculties.

Appointments and Promotions

While the trustees should leave all selection of new staff members, and all promotions, wholly to the president and deans, they should concern themselves with the *policies* relative to new appointments and promotions.

Nothing is much more objectionable or more detrimental to morale and academic standards than trustee-dictated appointments to the staff. In fact it is rarely wise for any trustee to make any suggestions as to who should be appointed, promoted, or discharged. A suggestion from a trustee is often misinterpreted as an order.

On the other hand, a sound policy on these matters, fixed by the trustees, if they hold the president to the policy, can be most helpful. In another place the tenure of the president has been discussed. Here, however, it is well to note that every president who is retained too long shows his failing usefulness early in acquiescing in undesirable appointments and unwarranted promotions and in retaining too long unpromising teachers. It is a very common experience for a newly appointed president to find on the staff a considerable number of members who are of relatively little value, but who have been retained so long that it is difficult to drop them or secure them other employment.

Two vital points of policy that should be followed are:

(1) To appoint or promote no one to a professorship or associate professorship without the most careful scrutiny and the confident opinion that in ability and personality, in success in teaching or in research, or in both, he is the man desired as a permanent member of the staff.

(2) To retain no instructor or assistant professor more than three or six years unless it is definitely planned to retain him permanently.

The crucial point in building a strong staff is in employing only very capable persons in the lower positions. If a high standard is maintained at the bottom it insures able young men of proven ability and personality for promotion, and relative ease in securing positions elsewhere for those who cannot be promoted.

There are a great number of teachers with the appropriate degrees and unobjectionable character who lack personality, enthusiasm, and vigor which a successful teacher must have. These teachers usually grow less useful with time, and they give little to students. If appointed to lower positions, they could certainly be identified in a few years and should not be retained. Far too many of such teachers are on the staff of every institution.

If the trustees called for a discriminating report on all staff members each year, it would go a long way to keep the executive up to the mark in this vital matter. Staff members in each of the usual four grades (professor, associate professor, assistant professor, instructor) can be rather readily grouped in three classifications:

1. Those who are so valuable that they cannot be replaced for the same salary and who should be considered for promotion or salary increase. This group usually includes a few persons who are so useful and so loyal and who have so woven their lives into the fabric of the institution that no one could replace them.

2. Those who could be replaced at the same salary, but probably could not be bettered at that salary. The assumption is that they should be retained without promotion or salary increase, unless they are instructors or assistant professors, and have reached the term limit of employment and so should be promoted or assisted to an appointment elsewhere.

3. Those who could be replaced by more valuable staff members at the same or a lower salary and who should presumably be replaced.

If the trustees' committee on teachers, by whatever name it may be called, would give one day each spring to such a report and a discussion with the president of what he proposes to do in promotions and in the removal and replacement of the least useful staff members, much good might be accomplished. It is not intended here to suggest that any action should be taken by the trustee committee or by the trustees as a body. They should not encroach upon the president's prerogative to recommend appointments and dismissals. However, such a meeting and discussion as outlined above would certainly keep the character and effectiveness of the staff members prominently in the president's mind and would result in a much stronger staff over a period of years. The temptation to the deans and president is to let things drift, and especially so as the time of their expected retirement approaches. A drifting policy always results in losing the ablest and keeping those who should be removed and so steadily weakens the staff.

The less valuable staff member in the lower ranks who is retained eight or ten years, and all associate and full professors have a strong case against dismissal. The trustees should concern themselves to see that staff members liable to dismissal later do not get into the higher ranks or overstay their appointments in lower ranks.

College professors esteem very highly the permanence of their positions. Usually more is lost in morale than is gained in strength in dealing summarily with staff members retained too long through executive neglect.

Another matter the trustees can well query is whether every vacancy needs to be filled. The tendency of college and university deans and presidents is always to fill vacancies. Often this is not the wisest plan. A policy of constant inquiry on the part of the trustees into the desirability of filling vacancies will in the long run increase efficiency and economy.

Except for serious specific offense it is very rarely wise to dismiss a staff member on short notice. The president, acting for the trustees, employed him. He must be as good as when he was employed. If he does not fit this institution permanently, it is probable he can find another that would better appreciate his services if he is given time. His employment was a mistake of the employing institution, and so it can well give ample notice and bear with him until he secures other employment. A considerate policy in such cases amply justifies itself.

The responsibility of an institution for the advancement of its younger staff members appears to deserve more consideration than it usually receives. No institution can promote all younger men. As a rule many more of the rank of instructor are employed than can possibly be promoted. As an illustration, in one institution employing 120 with the rank of instructor, only 10 are promoted each year on an average. The others are not re-employed after three to six years.

While, of course, many leave after a few years for further graduate work, for better teaching posts elsewhere, or for other reasons, there is usually no systematic assumption of responsibility for the employment of these younger men.

It would seem to be a sound and fruitful policy for an institution to obligate itself to either retain the services of young staff members, or secure satisfactory employment for them elsewhere. Such a policy, carefully pursued over a period of years, would materially improve the quality of men called to instructorships, improve the quality of assistant professors promoted from instructors, and materially increase the loyalty and enthusiasm of the younger men. It would also make the post of instructor at the institution more attractive to able young men.

The position of instructor at from $1,500 to $4,000 a year is recognized as a temporary appointment. Unfortunately, many department heads and deans, conscious of the temporary nature of these appointments, do not give their best efforts to securing the best possible men, and often appoint men lacking in personality, ability, or interest in teaching. These instructors usually teach full-time, and the appointment of an inferior man is always a calamity for the students. Such men are not usually reappointed, and drift away to what they can get.

Further, as the appointment of an instructor is temporary, it is exceptional for a department head to make any special effort to develop and improve his skill as a teacher. This results again in less skillful teaching than could be secured.

If it were the understood policy of the institution on employing a young instructor that he would be promoted or placed in a position elsewhere, distinct pressure would at once be felt by the dean and the department head, first, to secure as able and personable a man as possible, and second, to develop him into a good teacher so that he could be promoted or strongly recommended for a desirable post elsewhere.

If a department head, on the arrival of a new instructor, would ask him to select one of the best teachers in the department as his adviser, with the understanding that they would each visit the other's classes, and that they would discuss teaching problems and methods freely, a great deal could be done to correct the faults and improve the skill of a young teacher. At the same time the department head would have at hand an experienced professor who would know at first hand what quality of teaching the instructor was doing and what promise he had.

An astonishing amount of dull, uninspiring, and inexpert teaching that is unnecessary is being tolerated in most colleges and universities. Much of it is done by young, inexperienced teachers, who are given no help or suggestions by the able teachers.

Salaries

In a small college where the staff is small, if the salary limit is low and close to a minimum living wage, say if the average full professor's salary can only be $2,500 or $3,000, all full professors should receive the same salary. With such low salaries the spirit of the faculty is better if all share alike.

As salaries rise above a minimum living standard in the locality, differentiation can be introduced. Differences in salaries are generally based on length of service, if the maximum is not above $4,000. For example an associate or assistant professor may be promoted to the rank of full professor at $3,000 with an automatic increase of $200 every three years to a maximum of $3,600 after nine years' service.

In a large institution with higher salary limits, it is common to make salary increases based on the value of the man in teaching and research. Naturally in such cases the person who is both an outstanding teacher and a research man of distinction will receive the highest salary.

In any college or university much friction due to jealousy can be avoided by great care in the fair adjustment of salaries. To this end it is rarely sound practice to employ both a man and his wife. Their joint income from the college lifts their income well above that of their associates and may easily provoke serious contrasts with the ease of living of associates of the same rank.

Inasmuch as the value and distinction of any college depends almost wholly on the quality, ability, and personality of the faculty members, the administration of the institution by trustees and president should be steadily bent toward paying the highest salaries possible and securing the ablest men these salaries will command. No occasion should be given for a reputation that new buildings, athletic success, or any other matter is valued above the faculty. Wherever the athletic coach receives more than a full professor, this question is at once raised with cause.

It may be illuminating to say a word about the higher salaries being paid in our universities and colleges. There are 1,880 colleges and universities with 1,880 executive officers and over 140,000 on the teaching staffs. The following estimates are based in part on exact knowledge and in part on general knowledge and conversations with others; they are believed to be fairly accurate and conservative.

Among the higher paid university and college presidents:

35–45 receive salaries from $15,000 up to $30,000.

50–100 receive salaries of $12,000 to $14,000.

200 receive salaries of $9,000 to $10,000.

1,500 receive salaries of $5,000 to $9,000.

Among the higher paid university and college professors:

300 receive $10,000 to $12,000 or more.

500 receive $8,000 to $10,000.

2,000 receive $6,000 to $8,000.

20,000 receive $5,000 to $6,000.

Of the 140,000 on the staffs of our colleges and universities, excluding the presidents, over 15 per cent receive $5,000 or more.

There is a general idea among college teachers that they are poorly paid. It is certainly true that all people in this service have very high standards of living. They must dress reasonably well; they are hospitably inclined; their tastes in house furnishings call for good things; travel and books are much needed; adequate life insurance is felt necessary; certainly, they have many worthy uses for a good deal more money than they usually receive. If, however, we recall that the total income of half the families in the United States in 1948 was below $2,900; that $5,000 a year places a family among the wealthiest 12 per cent, college teachers do not fare so badly. While the most successful doctors and lawyers certainly receive much larger incomes than college professors, their expenses are much higher, and their lives are much more strenuous and much less under their own control. It is certainly true that few people live and work among pleasanter associates, or more nearly work along the lines of their own special interests than college teachers. It might also be added that many of the less valuable men are paid more than they earn.

Teaching Load

The question of what constitutes a reasonable teaching load in college and university has been much discussed. It is evident that in teaching, as in any other kind of work, a heavy overload is a mistake. A teacher with more students than he can teach well, instructs all poorly.

Of course some teachers can teach effectively more students than others. Some great teachers have directed and inspired very large classes to most effective work. This, however, has little bearing on the work an average college teacher can do.

In a college where teaching is the main work of the staff and research is a very minor matter, it is usually considered that 15 to 16 hours of classes a week is a full load. These classes ordinarily number thirty or less. Some colleges regard 12 hours as full work.

A teacher to do his best work cannot deal with too many different students if he is to meet them for individual, or small group conferences, which is often very desirable. The total number of students a teacher can deal with effectively seems to lie between 80 and 120, depending on the teacher and on the method of instruction.

It is evident that the teaching load depends on the number of classes met, and the number of students in the classes. We often call this student-class-hours. Four hours of class with 30 students would be 120 student-class-hours. Four hours of class with 8 students would be 32 student-class-hours. In a college, 300 to 350 student-class-hours is usually considered a full teaching load for an instructor who is free from other duties.

The work of different instructors varies greatly with the subject. An English teacher will have many essays to mark for spelling, punctuation, grammar, and style, meaning much work outside of class. A teacher of conversational French would have relatively little work outside class. Some courses require frequent conferences with individual students.

However, for a college as a whole it is reasonable to say that the teachers should carry on the average 300 student-class-hours per week. Most college students enroll for 15 or 16 hours a week. Therefore, 400 students would require $400 \times 15 = 6,000$ student-class-hours of instruction. If the curriculum could be so organized that each teacher on the average carried 300 hours, twenty teachers $(6,000/300 = 20)$ would be adequate, or one to each twenty students. However, it does not work out this way, because some courses like Latin, Greek, Philosophy, German, and others, if offered, usually enroll small classes. It is evident from the above that it is *possible* in a college to give good instruction with a staff of one teacher to twenty students. Just so far as the less popular subjects are included in the curriculum and as the range of subjects offered is increased above the minimum, the ratio drops.

It may prove interesting just here to give the actual ratio as determined from the statistics on enrollment for 1940 as reported by President Raymond Walters in *School and Society*, December 14, 1940. All the institutions included in Table 10 are of the undergraduate college type where there is small emphasis on research or graduate work.

From Table 10 it is evident that very few colleges are operated with a minimum faculty. The larger faculty is provided partly to increase the offerings of the curriculum and give students a wider selection of subjects, and partly to provide instruction in physical education and athletics, music, and other subjects giving little or no academic credit. Both

TABLE 10
STUDENT-FACULTY RATIO

Number of Colleges	Number Enrolled	Average Enrolled	Ave. No. Teachers	Ratio Students to Teachers	Extreme Numbers of Students per Teachers
26......	86 to 194	161	28.5	5.75 to 1	3.92 to 12
63......	200 – 299	254	31.7	8.3 – 1	4.8 – 14.6
84......	300 – 399	347	35.2	9.85 – 1	4.5 – 16.9
70......	400 – 499	447	37.9	11.8 – 1	6.8 – 20
43......	500 – 599	552	47.7	11.7 – 1	7.1 – 27.6
34......	600 – 699	653	54.4	12.0 – 1	5.9 – 25.1
23......	700 – 799	755	72.0	10.5 – 1	6.8 – 16.7
14......	800 – 899	844	67	12.6 – 1	8.5 – 19.9
7......	900 – 999	930	65.7	14.1 – 1	10 – 17.7
8......	1,000 – 1,099	1,049	85.8	12.2 – 1	8.3 – 19.4
15......	1,100 – 1,499	1,250	97.7	12.8 – 1	7.1 – 23.4
8......	1,500 – 1,999	1,665	126.0	13.2 – 1	8.1 – 17.0
7......	2,000 – 2,999	2,255	150.4	14.9 – 1	8.8 – 21.5
2......	6,688 – 7,008	6,848	563	12.2 – 1	....

reasons are good, but it should be remembered that increasing the staff is done by paying lower salaries and presumably getting less able teachers. Bearing all things in mind it seems reasonable to suggest that the objective of the trustees of a college with limited resources might be set at a ratio of fifteen students per teacher, with a maximum teaching load of 350 student-class-hours, and an average for the whole staff of 225.

In a university or in an institution however named in which there is large emphasis on research, the teaching load is usually lighter. The calculation is difficult because there are so many part-time instructors and also those who do not teach at all but give their time to research. On the other hand, these institutions are usually large, enrolling from 2,000 to 20,000 students, and there are very few small classes except at the graduate, or senior college-graduate level. Here many teachers can well carry a full load of 300–350 student-clock-hours, while many others will of necessity carry much lighter loads, those teaching graduate students only, perhaps averaging 120. For the whole institution an average of 200 to 225 student-clock-hours might be regarded as reasonable.

In most universities, from 8 to 12 hours of teaching a week is regarded as a full teaching load for a professor who engages in research. The truth is that when such a standard is set up many claim it as a reasonable load when they really do little outside of teaching. It is reasonable anywhere to expect a teacher giving little or no time to research, administration, or other outside duty to instruct classes from 12 to 16 hours a week.

A good university teacher, like any good worker, expects to put into his job about 45 hours of work a week. Many work from 50 to 75 hours a week. This will be distributed between some or all of the following duties: classroom instruction, conferences with students, preparing lectures and classroom discussions, reading papers and reports, research and writing, reading current journals in his fields, administrative duties, attending examinations for advanced degrees, attending committee meetings and faculty meetings. The duties of no two men are the same.

The evaluation of research work is very difficult. Relatively few men in even our greatest institutions are really men of great research ability. Those who really are able research investigators should have as ample time for this work as possible. On the other hand, it is undesirable to release men of indifferent research ability from other work on account of research. It is difficult to discriminate sharply between the two types of men, but it is too often true that much university time is spent in research by men of indifferent ability who will yield meagre returns.

The trustees could well define some policies relative to teaching load, research, and administrative work, that would strengthen the hands of the deans and president in administering the intricate work of a university.

As a general standard the following may be considered reasonable maximum teaching loads: for one who teaches only graduate students, 120 student-class-hours; for one who teaches only juniors and seniors, 240 student-class-hours; for one who teaches only freshmen and sophomores, 360 student-class-hours. Where one teaches in two or three of these areas an intermediate figure would be reasonable.

It can well be suggested at this point that it is most desirable for the president to study reports on small classes each term. There is always a strong tendency for professors to sanction small classes. Some must be given. However, constant pressure by the president against small classes, except where they are clearly necessary, will greatly reduce the number and will save a surprisingly large sum in salaries.

Sabbatical Leave

"Sabbatical leave" is generally accepted as meaning leave of absence, one year in seven on full salary, for study. However, many modifications of this are in operation.

Any professor, fully engaged in his work, year after year, is likely to settle to a routine, and he may allow his teaching to grow out of date. The younger men on the staff—instructors and assistant professors—are fresh from the universities, but the older men—professors and associate professors—are usually a good many years away from this stimulus. If wisely administered, an occasional leave of absence on pay, granted to the permanent staff members, is well repaid by better service.

While leave on full salary for one full year every seven years is ideal and most desirable, it is beyond the means of most institutions. The cheapest modification is leave on half salary. Usually with some reorganization of the work for the year, a young substitute can be secured for not much more than the other half of the salary regularly paid. This costs the college practically nothing, and while half-pay is inadequate for most professors with a family, it is often a great boon to eager scholars, and occasionally may be supplemented by foundation grants in aid.

Some institutions offer the option of a half year on full pay or a whole year on half pay. The former plan will cost the institution for a substitute about one-fourth the professor's salary, and the latter practically nothing.

Various other modifications result in economies to institutions obliged to regard them. Some institutions grant leave of absence one year in ten or twelve. Some adopt a rule that only two or three professors may be granted leave on pay in the same year. Such regulations avoid any heavy expense in any one year for leaves of absence.

There should always be a clear understanding that a sabbatical leave is not a vacation, but a period for increasing the value of the service of the individual to the institution. A wise restriction is to require the professor eligible for leave to submit to the president his plans for spending his leave, for approval by the trustees.

Whether the time is to be spent at some center or centers of learning in study or research, or in travel for some specific scholarly aim, it should stand the consideration and win the approval of the president and the trustees. A sabbatical leave devoted to golf and swimming at a winter resort scarcely conforms with the purpose of the leave.

The trustees of every institution could well study this matter and try to devise some plan under which at least some members of their teaching staff could occasionally leave their routine duties for some contact with other centers of learning.

Retirement

Retirement at 65, 68, or 70 from full teaching and administrative duties is now the general rule. While occasionally a man maintains his full intellectual power and value beyond these ages, it is more and more widely recognized that at 65 he has earned the right to relief from the strenuous demands of full responsibility. Also in the great majority of cases, work suffers if full regular work is expected of a man over 65 or 70.

In fact, an administration should have the authority to retire teachers from full work at any time over 60 if their failing usefulness warrants.

A problem of increasing importance in America, as retirement of all professors at 65–70 becomes more common, is the best way to utilize the value of men in retirement. While many men cease to be useful at 65 or earlier, many still have great powers, and while certainly they should give way to younger men, their value should be utilized as far as possible. It is certainly desirable to provide retired staff members with offices or at least desk room, and encourage them to continue to write or carry on research. To be of any creative or productive value it is usually essential for them to retain an effective academic connection, and usually the institution will profit by providing this connection.

The trustees should define a policy relative to retirement of staff members. Possibly the most satisfactory plan allows retirement for cause after 60, optional retirement of teachers at 65, and obligatory retirement at 68 or 70.

In the case of all administrative officers obligatory retirement from *administrative* duties should be not later than 65. In many cases administrative duties should be surrendered earlier. In all of these cases the individual should be transferred to other work, where his services will be most useful and his presence will in no way be an embarrassment to his successor.

Pensions and Other Provisions for Retirement

As it is impossible to drop faithful employees in their old age without some financial provision, and as old age pensions are now generally paid in all fields of employment, the problem of pensions is closely tied up with the retirement policy.

Pensions are almost universally paid for jointly by the professor and the institution, 4 per cent or 5 per cent of the professor's salary being deducted monthly and the institution contributing approximately the same amount. Roughly 10 per cent of the salary compounded for 35 or 40 years will pay an annuity of about half the *average* salary on which 10 per cent has been paid. It is exceptional for a pension of over $3,500 to be paid.

Pensions are generally financed through the Insurance Department of the Carnegie Foundation for the Advancement of Teaching. They can be financed as above through any insurance company. Where a pension system is in force every member of the regular teaching staff should be obliged to participate.

In those states having a state teachers' retirement system open to teachers in the state university and colleges, teachers are usually retired on the basis of teachers in the public school system with a maximum pension of $1,000 to $1,200. In some states enjoying this arrangement the state institutions provide some supplementary pensions.

In some institutions where pensions are not provided, staff members at from 65 to 70 are put on half-time work and half pay, the work being adjusted among teaching, research, and administration so as best to accommodate the individual and the institution. This plan has the definite advantage of retaining the older men in close connection with the institution. In case this plan is followed, a pension should be provided at age 75, as the value of men beyond this age cannot be large. Such a system, of half-time work and half pay from 68 or 70 to 75, with a pension of $1,200 to $1,500 after 75, would not be costly and would prove acceptable at many institutions unable to adopt a more generous policy.

The trustees should certainly adopt some policy under which older teachers who cease to be useful can be relieved of their duties with dignity.

Insurance. In many institutions today the institution, alone or on a participating basis, carries group insurance on all staff members. This usually provides insurance equal to the teacher's annual salary. Additional insurance, up to twice this amount, may be carried at the expense of the insured. Usually the maximum allowed is not over $10,000.

Efficiency of Deans and Heads of Departments

A great deal depends on the leadership, helpfulness, and sympathetic understanding of deans and heads of departments. Much depends also upon their ability to judge and encourage good teaching and valuable research. In many, many cases throughout the country, departments and colleges are seriously handicapped by men in positions of leadership who do not lead.

These administrative positions are too often regarded as permanent positions. A new attitude ought to be built up, emphasizing the professorship as the permanent post and the administrative work as necessary and very important but not permanent, the appointee holding the post while his services prove highly useful there, but returning to his previous rank of professor when his service in administration becomes less useful. Such a transfer back to the professorship should not be regarded as a demotion, but as a relief from burdensome administrative work; and as a reward for services rendered, the salary drawn as dean or department head should, if possible, be continued to the age of retirement. At least, the monthly salary paid for 12 months to the dean should be continued for 9 months to the dean who returns to a porfessorship. This salary arrangement will take most of the sting out of giving up the administrative work, and the increased freedom it will give the president in replacing the least valuable administrative officers with abler men will be very cheap at the price.

Again and again one familiar with higher education finds departments of ten to thirty or more members, employed at an expense of $25,000 to $100,000, limping along inefficiently because of poor or inadequate leadership. With an able, competent, acceptable leader the level of work will be greatly raised.

Not only is the efficiency and enthusiasm of the whole institution immensely improved by competent leadership, but the young staff members who are *entitled* to good and helpful leadership profit by it. Trustees rarely appreciate their responsibility, when authorizing the employment of young teachers at low salaries, to give these teachers adequate and capable leadership to stimulate and develop their best abilities.

Inevitably and properly in large institutions a considerable part of the responsibility for new appointments to the staff falls on department heads and deans of colleges. Unless these posts are held by able, active men, who are keenly aware of the great importance of securing the best possible men, many vacancies will be filled by persons of inferior ability, poor personality, and of small value as teachers. It is always hard to find and secure the best man available at a given salary. The most desirable men are rarely hunting new positions. They are busy with their present work. It is tiresome to canvass the whole country for a first-class man when by writing to an agency or to a few institutions, a man can be found with the proper degrees who may be passable. Again and again in studying new appointments in institutions, persons are found who are far below the best who are available at the salary. This fault reflects not only on the president, but largely on deans and department heads.

To the end that the leadership throughout the institution may be maintained at the highest possible level, the trustees should have an annual rating of all administrative officers similar to that described for teachers, and the president should be pressed to replace each year those deans and department heads who are not giving a service of high value. It is always an unpleasant and difficult duty to remove deans and department heads, and unless pressed to it by the trustees, it is far easier to allow ineffective leaders to remain. Nothing is more detrimental to the institution. Ineffective administrative heads mean poor appointments under them, unwise promotions, and various sins of commission and omission that destroy morale and weaken the services of the staff.

A system that is democratic and at the same time helps overcome the difficulty of reducing a dean to a professor is the one under which the faculty, working with the president or provost, elect the deans for four- or five-year terms. At the end of his term, a dean may be re-elected, he may retire, or he may be replaced. This system works well at Ohio State University.

It is certainly an important responsibility of the trustees to adopt policies which will insure a high level of leadership in deans and department heads, and in the various administrative posts in the business offices.

Tenure and Academic Freedom

This is one of the most widely discussed subjects in the academic world. It is essential that trustees and administrative officers understand the points at issue.

To this end it would be most profitable to read "The Statement of Principles, 1940, of Academic Freedom and Tenure" in the *Bulletin of the American Association of University Professors*, Vol. XXVII, pages 40–45, as well as the discussion of "Academic Freedom and Tenure" by Henry M. Wriston, president of Brown University, in Vol. XXV, pages 328–43 of the same publication.

The usual ranking of college and university teachers is in four grades: professors, associate professors, assistant professors, and instructors. In the best practice professors and associate professors are employed for life or until the accepted retirement age. Usually assistant professors are appointed for a term of two, three, or six years. At the end of this period,

by giving due notice of at least three months, it is understood that the institution can properly terminate the appointment. Instructors are usually appointed for one or two years
at a time, with the understanding that unless they win promotion within a stated time, usually three to six years, their
connection with the institution automatically terminates.

The status of the assistant professor and instructor becomes
greatly confused when either is continued in employment beyond six years. Their positions are not usually regarded as
permanent, but continued employment tends to give them
permanent status. Harvard University proposes to make no
further appointments to the rank of assistant professor and
promote instructors directly to the rank of associate professors. The Association of University Professors in the "Statement of Principles" cited above, urges that after a probationary
period of not to exceed six years, a full-time instructor or
assistant professor is entitled to permanent status.

On the whole there is sound reason in these several practices. It is inexcusable for a man to be appointed to a professorship or associate professorship until he is recognized as
an experienced teacher, until he has made a record of his
ability in teaching and research, of his attitudes and character.
It is assumed that before a man is appointed to such important
positions, he has been fully investigated and that the institution
is satisfied with him. Such a man usually has a satisfactory
position when he is invited to accept a professorship or associate professorship, and there is sound reason to suppose that
the institution calling him is offering him a permanent post.
Harvard fully recognized this responsibility. It is stated in
the University Catalogue that professors and associate professors are permanently appointed. No man holding such
posts at Harvard has been dismissed for many years.

Usually when trouble arises about such appointments it is
due to one of four causes:

1. The appointment was made without adequate investigation. The dean or president responsible failed to find out what sort of man he was appointing. The institution was responsible. Later undesirable characteristics in the appointee were discovered and the appointment was regretted.

2. The appointment made under one administration did not meet the approval of the succeeding administration. The new dean or president finds the appointee unsatisfactory and wishes him removed.

3. Occasionally a professor who was satisfactory when appointed, changes as years pass, either through developing an attitude offensive to the administration on some current matter, or through neglect of his work, and becomes undesirable on the staff.

4. The professor makes statements in class or in public addresses which are offensive to the president or trustees, and which they regard as seriously prejudicial to the interests of the institution. Statements at which offense is taken are usually in the fields of religion, politics, and social science. It is this last cause which has produced most discussion and embarrassment.

Every professor feels that he has the right and the duty to teach his subject in the classroom as he understands it, and as he believes it to be the truth. He also feels that as a citizen he has the right to speak in public as he pleases. In both points he is correct so long as he is restrained by common sense, and a feeling for the fitness of things a gentleman should recognize.

If the expression of certain views is not tolerated by an institution, it should be made clear in writing at the time of discussing the appointment. Very few professors would accept appointment where ideas they cherished were not acceptable. On the other hand many professors have made unnecessarily irritating statements on subjects outside their special fields.

It is generally true that a reasonably thorough investigation of the man by the institution before appointment will avoid the difficulty.

It should be noted here that such difficulty rarely occurs with a man who has risen through the ranks by promotion and who fully understands the college and its ideals. It usually occurs with men brought in from other institutions with advanced rank. This again emphasizes the desirability of great care in selecting men for the lower positions and filling advanced positions by promotion wherever possible.

Considering that there are 1,880 colleges and universities in the country employing over 140,000 teachers, it seems probable that relatively few teachers are dismissed unfairly. However, Harvard and quite a number of other institutions feel that more harm results to the institution by dismissing seemingly undesirable men than by retaining them. It is believed that the absolute certainty of appointments and entire freedom from fear of dismissal adds more to the efficiency of the staff as a whole than the replacement of an occasional undesirable teacher by a superior man. It is probably true also that in institutions comparable with Harvard in academic standards, there is great social pressure within the staff itself to keep a man in conformity with accepted standards.

While it is true that every institution should earnestly endeavor to follow the example of our old and leading institutions in making all appointments with great care and regarding such appointments as sacred obligations, it is undoubtedly true that many institutions fail to do so.

Among such public institutions in which political pressure bears on the university, and among colleges which have, or have had, incompetent executives, situations often develop in which occasional dismissals of professors seem inevitable. Usually the men dismissed from such institutions should look upon it as a fortunate release, but this is not always the case.

Such dismissals are usually traceable to politics or unwise appointments by incompetent executives. They certainly always reflect unfavorably on the institution.

Usually such dismissals can be avoided by a full acceptance of responsibility by the institution. If the president frankly tells the individual that he does not wish to retain him permanently, but that he will be retained until he can find another post, the professor in question will usually secure other employment within a few years.

It should certainly be the policy of trustees to maintain the permanency of appointment of professors and associate professors. Any tendency to violate it should raise a serious question as to the wisdom and judgment of the president.

Instructors usually have the masters or doctors degree, and little or no teaching experience when appointed. An appointment as instructor is definitely a temporary appointment at a relatively small salary. However, it has very often happened that an annual appointment has been repeated again and again until the recipient is a fixture as an instructor at a very low salary. It is due to a recognition of this frequent occurrence that within recent years it has become increasingly common to make these appointments for 1, 2, or 3 years with a fixed limit beyond which an instructor may not serve, unless he is promoted in rank. Three to six years are the common periods of service of an instructor. At the end of this period four alternatives are possible: he may be promoted, he may obtain an appointment at another institution at the same or higher rank, he may return to graduate school for further study, or he may drop out of the teaching profession.

It is the responsibility of the trustees to assure themselves that weak, inadequate teachers are not permanently retained as instructors. In some instances it seems wise to try to retain good teachers with the rank of instructor. It would seem however, that a really capable teacher on permanent appointment should receive a reasonable salary, and if he is intentionally retained permanently with rank of instructor, his salary should be above that of the grade.

Assistant professors are neither inexperienced teachers, as many instructors must be, nor are they usually men of established reputation as teachers and research workers. Instructors of marked promise are promoted in rank to assistant professors and receive a salary between that of an instructor and an associate professor. Their appointment is customarily for some fixed period, usually three years. It is accepted as good practice to limit reappointment to a second three-year term, six years in all. If no opening for promotion develops, the assistant professor is given ample notice and is expected to find another opening elsewhere at the end of his term.

The promotion to an assistant professorship is an encouragement and a challenge. It is supposed to be an opportunity for a promising young teacher to prove himself. If he really does prove himself to be an able person, promotion in his own institution or elsewhere is pretty sure to follow.

The trustees should assure themselves that a sound, fair policy relative to teachers in this rank is being carried out, that every appointee understands his status in tenure and in department esteem each year.

Relative to the whole matter of tenure it may be said that where the president and deans are competent and keep themselves fully informed about the work and status of each staff member, trouble rarely develops. It is usually the result of negligence, hasty, thoughtless action, lack of consideration for others, or stupidity.

Academic Freedom

Freedom of speech is such an important matter to a college teacher, and today it is given so little thought by most people, that it warrants some further discussion. In the United States speech is ordinarily so very free that most people accept it as they accept air and light, without any thought. They express any opinion that comes to mind freely, and thoughtlessly, regardless of its effect.

Today college and university teachers, clergymen, and newspaper correspondents are the only classes of people whose employment is likely to be placed in peril through saying what they think in discharging the duties of their employment.

Formerly it was the church itself which put people to death who made statements contrary to established teachings. More recently the wealthy exerted their powerful influence to suppress those who opposed great concentrations of wealth. Socialistic, communistic, and anti-church views still arouse strong antagonism. It is only under our modern dictators, however, that freedom of speech has been entirely stifled.

The college and university teacher, dealing with fairly mature students, and urged continually to teach the truth and teach the students to think, resents most emphatically any check on his freedom to state and discuss the truth as he sees it in his own field. He maintains that the college is the national custodian of the truths of the ages and of the most recently discovered truths; that it is his special duty to pass on the truth to the youth of the land; that only his peers in his own field of knowledge are competent to judge his statements.

In mathematics, physics, chemistry, geology, and astronomy, free expression is not now questioned. In zoology and botany, and in Greek, Latin, French, German, and other foreign languages and literature, speech is relatively free. But in religion, philosophy, economics, sociology, history, government, and psychology, many people think they know enough to judge truth from error, and they are quick to take exception to opinions differing from their own.

These very fields in which our knowledge is less exact, where we know relatively less than in the sciences, where further advances are most needed by society, is where freedom of speech is most often denied. It is essential that our most able men search out the truth in these fields. It is on the discovery and effective application of the truth in these fields that our very civilization and the life of our race depend. Here, also, men must feel free to work and think and speak. Mistakes must be made and corrected, theories must be stated to be proved wrong. Here, as in the sciences, many mistakes must be made and many wrong theories defended, before the truth emerges. What we do not know about government, money, trade, business, human relations, labor and capital, and international relations, is proved on every hand by the terrible state of the whole world. We must discover the truth in all these fields, painful though it may be.

It is gratifying that among so many institutions and so many teachers, so few are under criticism. It speaks well for the wisdom and judgment of both the teachers and the trustees. Usually, as long as teachers confine their discussions to the field of their specialization, they are guarded in their statements by their earnest desire to be accurate. Teachers, like other people, speak most freely where their knowledge is less complete, and on the border of their field they are more likely to make statements really open to criticism.

Trustees do well to respect freedom of speech and not to bring pressure for the dismissal of teachers on such grounds as are discussed above. The reputation of an institution for academic freedom is more valuable than a reputation for restricted teaching. While occasionally a thoughtless professor makes a foolish and unfortunate statement, it is soon forgotten. There is always so much good and so much strength in every college that nothing much can injure it seriously except limiting freedom of speech or political control.

The Private Employment of Faculty Members

The private employment of faculty members has many

different angles, and many varying attitudes toward it are maintained.

Massachusetts Institute of Technology, our greatest and most distinguished engineering school and technological institute, always has been proud of the considerable number of her staff retained by important firms as consultants. In many cases salaries and teaching loads have been adjusted to the convenience of the distinguished professors who have elected to carry on teaching and consultation side by side. There has been a distinct advantage to the teacher in thus keeping close to the latest developments in the field.

In medicine this has been a source of much discussion. As now conducted, most of our best medical schools employ many men on a full-time basis, with no private practice; some men, especially surgeons and certain distinguished specialists, are employed on a part-time basis with the privilege of accepting a certain amount of private practice.

It seems evident that no hard and fast rule will work in this field. Many college teachers are devoting their time to fields of knowledge where little, if any, outside employment could be obtained. Others, quite the opposite, have increasing requests for services because of their employment by the university. In the case of some men, any outside employment will merely detract from the time and attention they give to their teaching, without in any way increasing their value as teachers. Others, through outside employment, gain experience and information of great value in keeping their teaching up to high quality.

It is, generally speaking, wise to so arrange with men who are allowed to carry outside employment along with teaching, that the disproportion of income is not too great. For example, a man employed at full salary and giving three-fourths of his time to outside employment from which he receives a large income would certainly bring serious discontent to his associates. If the services of such a man are to be retained, it should certainly be on a part-time basis of both time and salary.

All such cases call for careful handling. Certainly the institution must not be exploited for private profit, and the contentment of the faculty should be guarded. However where the services of such a man are needed and where all his time cannot be secured, the president and the trustees should have the courage to work out a sound, tenable basis for his employment.

Research Foundations

One more matter seems fittingly placed in this chapter, the manner of handling patents in our larger institutions where much research is carried on. More and more frequently in recent years, discoveries are made by faculty members that could well result in patents. How should patents be handled?

Seventy-seven institutions have established research foundations empowered to handle patents and all expense and income resulting. To function usefully these foundations should be legally incorporated, operate under a board of directors, and have a thoroughly competent secretary. Much will depend on the activity and judgment of the secretary. As the foundation continues from year to year, a considerable amount of time will be necessary for the secretary to adequately handle the business that arises. In one instance, in ten years since organization a college research foundation has an annual income of $20,000 and requires about three hours' work a day by the secretary. A number of others have much larger incomes.

All patents are taken in the name of the foundation, and all cost and expense in securing and defending patents is borne by the foundation. Rules are set up relative to the income from patents. In most cases there is no income, in some a good deal. Under certain conditions, the member of the staff making the invention involved receives a certain per cent of the income.

Inasmuch as there is always a probability of an attack on the patent or an infringement, it seems wise to set aside a reserve from the income from each patent of perhaps 10 per cent to cover these costs. When any reserve accumulates to $10,000, that should be adequate in most cases, and further accumulation could be discontinued.

A great institution, spending in excess of 2 million dollars a year on research, and many spending less, discovers all kinds of things. Many, perhaps the large majority, are in no way adapted to patents. Some, while not promising any considerable income, should be patented and made free to the public to prevent some private concern from taking a patent and exploiting the public. A certain small percentage of discoveries made by members of the staff, on time paid for by the institution and with equipment and supplies paid for by the institution, are both subject to patent and produce considerable income if sold or licensed to private industrial concerns. Over the years these research foundations take in an increasing income which, under the regulations of the foundations, is all spent for further research.

Such foundations, if wisely managed, not only bring in considerable sums for the enlarged support of research, but they relieve the faculty members of costs, of all the responsibilities and business worries involved, and on the whole protect the good name of the university and the private interests of the professor. It seems probable that, in spite of some unfavorable criticism from highly placed men in our universities, increasing numbers of research foundations will be established.

CHAPTER 12

THE LIBRARY

THE library must at all times be the center of the intellectual life of a college or university, from which the accumulated knowledge of the ages flows freely to each department. If the library is inadequately financed, or if its administration is ineffective in making all its resources easily available, the flow of knowledge, past and present, is impeded or wholly cut off from some or from many departments. Unless each department can draw easily and surely, according to its needs, on such knowledge as an adequate library can supply, the institution cannot be maintained at a high level of service.

It at once becomes interesting to discover what is meant by a library adequate to the needs of the particular institution with which one is concerned. First it can be said that very rarely indeed is the library of an institution too good. Very rarely indeed is the support available so generous and the administration of the library so excellent that the library is superior in quality to the needs of the institution.

There are at least five requirements that any library must meet before it can be regarded as adequate in service. The larger the library the more important it is that each of these is met.

The Library Must Be Directed by a Competent Librarian

The best library administration is secured by appointing an able librarian and giving him full authority. If a library committee is appointed, the librarian should be chairman, provided he is competent. A good library committee can often aid the librarian in maintaining proper regulations and in a wise distribution of book purchases. In the large universities there is especially a need of a library representative of each important department who will be responsible for looking after the collection of important material in his department.

The librarian, like all administrative officers, should be the servant of the faculty, aiding them in the use of books. To do this he must often protect the faculty from some members who tend to be too demanding for their departments; he must keep a reasonable balance throughout the institution. He must see the library and its problems from outside, from the viewpoint of a library patron. He must see how the library can serve each patron most effectively and most conveniently. The routine librarian sees everything from the inside and from the viewpoint of the library worker. He opposes changes from routine. A real librarian will make any possible change in routine that will extend the effective use of books.

The librarian in a college, if fully competent, should be of the rank of a full professor. Usually, if it is impossible to pay the librarian a full professor's salary, it is wise either to arrange to secure a librarian who can teach part time, or to appoint as librarian a full professor who does teach but who would be most able properly to supervise the library, and give him trained librarians as assistants.

In a university the fully competent librarian should probably rank in position and salary with the deans. Unfortunately, in spite of the large number of persons trained in the different technical phases of library work, there are very few first-class librarians in the country. The supply is slowly increasing, and proper appreciation and recognition of the importance of first-class ability in this field will increase the supply. Even now a diligent search and an attractive salary can secure a good man. It cannot be overstressed that no library can be developed to service of high quality unless an able, informed, and adequately trained man is at the head.

While an equally competent woman may give excellent service in the library of a woman's college or of a small college, a man can usually deal much more easily and effectively with department heads and other influential library patrons.

More Must Be Spent for Salaries of the Staff Than for Books

In all except the smallest libraries more must be spent for the salaries of the librarian and his staff than for books and periodicals. In forty large university libraries the average is 40 per cent for books and periodicals and 60 per cent for salaries. In smaller libraries the ratio will be nearer 50–50.

This always strikes one as unreasonable on hearing it for the first time, but after considering all the work which must be done in a modern college library by the librarian and his staff, it is not so hard to understand. The work of the staff is chiefly made up of the following duties:

Buying new books.

Cataloguing.

Aiding students and faculty in finding what they need— reference work.

Issuing books and receiving returned books.

Receiving, checking, supervising periodicals.

Attending to binding of books and magazines.

Aiding the members of the faculty in selecting new books to be bought.

Consulting with faculty members in the preparation of lists for required and supplementary reading.

Representing the interests of the library in the faculty and on committees.

In an institution well served by the library, the annual use of books within and outside the library building will run from 100 to 150 books per student and faculty member. The total work in a library is surprisingly large, and an adequate, well-trained staff is necessary.

The Library Must Be Well Supported

To state definitely what it is wise for any particular institution to spend on its library is difficult, but the generally accepted standards are as follows:

In a junior college enrolling from 250 to 1,000 students, $10 per student per year is regarded as reasonably adequate. With a smaller enrollment it would be very desirable to increase this per capita allowance, if possible to $15. If the enrollment is 1,500 to 3,000, the per capita might reasonably be $7.50 or even $5.00.

In a liberal arts college 4 per cent of the total college budget, or $25 per student enrolled, is regarded generally as reasonable support for the library.

A university library differs chiefly from a college library in that the university must meet the demands of research for books and periodicals. The policy of the trustees in defining clearly the fields in which major research will be developed will have an important effect on expenditures. Inasmuch as the budgets of all institutions doing real university work are large, 4 per cent of the budget, or if the enrollment exceeds 8,000, $20 per student, will provide reasonably well for the library.

Forty of our leading universities spend for library books, periodicals, and binding, and for staff salaries, an average of 3.92 per cent of their entire budgets. The range is from 1.03 per cent to 8.5 per cent. Twenty-three spend from 2 per cent to 4.5 per cent, three spend less than 2 per cent, and twelve more than 4.5 per cent. The two factors that necessarily push up the library cost are, first, departmental libraries—the more and the better they are administered the higher the cost; second, the number of fields in which major research work is pursued. In every such field probably over 80 per cent of all important material in all languages should be available in the library, and this involves the purchase of many periodicals in complete files and current subscriptions.

The Chief Object of the Library Administration Must Be to Have the Books Used

While formerly the chief function of the library was to keep and preserve the books, now it is to secure the widest possible use of the books. Reference librarians aid students and faculty in securing the material they need. Every effort is made to familiarize the students with the resources of the library and how to find the books they wish. Unless the per capita book use is large, the library administration or the teaching methods of the institution must be at fault.

The Service at the Delivery Desk Must Be Prompt

If a student is forced to wait any considerable length of time at the desk for a book, he will be inclined to use the library as little as possible. In a well-run library not over 2 minutes should elapse between turning in a call slip and receiving the book, or being informed that the book is out. A wait of 5 to 8 minutes or more for a book greatly discourages the use of the library.

A library which scores high on each of the above five points is a good library.

While a library is primarily maintained for use, it is also a reservoir of knowledge.

As one looks into the use of books in any library he finds many new books and periodicals that have not been used at all or used extremely little. This suggests that many books have been purchased that are not needed. Of necessity much must be available that is not immediately needed. The trustees and administration, here as in other areas, must rely on the good judgment of a wise and well-informed librarian. A search of any large physical or chemical laboratory will always disclose large quantities of apparatus, equipment, and chemicals unused or used very little, or outmoded, or in reserve. Here we expect it. We must expect a similar situation also in the library.

There are a number of special library problems on which some things may be said of interest to the trustees.

Departmental Libraries

Departmental libraries are a desirable luxury. Our largest and richest institutions maintain these to great advantage. However, where funds are limited it is far preferable to have all books in one well-administered library, open from 8 A.M. to 10 P.M. There are two serious objections to departmental libraries when funds are limited. In the first place, library needs of departments are now so largely overlapping that unless duplicate copies are extensively provided for departmental libraries, great inconvenience will often result. Where funds permit the purchase of duplicate copies for departmental libraries, they are, of course, a great convenience. The second objection is that unless funds are available to provide the service of competent librarians for department libraries, the service there is usually poor, the hours the library is open are short, and the loss of valuable books is large. But if funds are available for adequate service the department library is very useful.

Since in the vast majority of college and university libraries, support is below minimum requirements, it is generally to everyone's advantage to concentrate on one library, containing all the books and giving the best possible service.

Reserve Books

Today many departments, especially those in the social sciences, require students to read extensively in certain library books usually kept in a room or on shelves designated "Reserve

Books." Such books are not taken outside the library except over night. Usually several duplicates of each of these books are necessary. Where funds are easily available, sufficient duplicate copies can be provided. Where funds are limited it is much more satisfactory to assess each student in a class using reserve books $1 a year and provide ample duplicates. These books are essentially textbooks, and it is entirely reasonable to require the students to pay for them.

Duplicate Copies

The purchase of duplicate copies must be left to the judgment of the librarian. Often a casual survey of a library discloses many copies of an outdated book, and its purchase seems to have been extravagant. However, this is a matter that must be left in the hands of the librarian.

Special Gifts

Libraries are often tendered gifts of books with the request that they be shelved together. It is an excellent rule to accept no gifts of books under any restrictions. A library can always accept unrestricted gifts of books, using what is valuable and disposing suitably of the remainder. Those used can be marked with a suitable book plate giving due credit to the donor. It is well to remember that the labor of cataloguing a book and the cost of shelf space is about $1 per book. Shelf space is always limited. Furthermore, the use of a book is increased materially by shelving it in its proper place according to its catalogue number. Collections given under shelving restrictions are expensive, awkward to use, and lead to bad library practice.

Microfilms and Microcards

Most libraries are now provided with equipment for making and reading microfilms and microcards, and for suitably preserving them. Their use is steadily increasing. Since they may

work a revolution in library policies and practice, trustees
should be familiar with the institution's needs in this respect.

Library Exchanges

Interlibrary loans of books are now commonplace. In
this way rare books can be procured for scholars needing them,
the library's services increased, and its purchasing obligations
lessened. As the volume of these interlibrary loans increase,
much saving in the purchase of rare and little used books will
result.

Of the making of books, and of technical periodicals, there
is no end. No library can possibly collect all material on all
subjects. The smaller college libraries should concentrate on
working collections. Rare books and specialized journals
should be bought with great care. The large university
libraries should agree on certain fields in which they will
collect exhaustively and not attempt to duplicate outstanding
collections in nearby cities. The fields of research are so many
and so important that even the greatest institutions should
decide where they wish to build and maintain outstanding
strength.

Probable Growth and the Library Building

The problem of providing adequate room for books faces
every library. In meeting this problem there are several
factors that should be kept in mind. It is highly improbable
that any good institution will ever buy fewer books annually
than it is buying now. Fields of knowledge are all growing,
needs for books are expanding. So if we multiply present
annual accessions by 50 or 100, a reasonable estimate is
obtained of the books that will be added in the next 50 or 100
years. Also it is most desirable so to locate and design the
library that the portion containing book stacks can be extended. Nothing, except poor administration, does more to
defeat the service of a library than overcrowding the stacks

with books. There should always be plenty of room on the shelves of the active collection. If adequate stack room is lacking it can be easily relieved by providing storage shelves in some available fireproof room, or by erecting a cheap building shell for storage stacks. In every library a relatively small fraction of the books is in active use. Many books which are too valuable to be discarded can well be placed in storage outside the library. A daily messenger service to this storeroom can procure all books called for with little delay. Usually such a storeroom is very much cheaper to provide than an addition to the library.

The library building, as it houses the institution's most important equipment, should be designed first to permit the most efficient service. Far too often a selfish donor and an architect ignorant of library needs plan a library which is beautiful as a building and a striking monument to the donor, but is most inefficient and unsatisfactory for library purposes. Certainly every library should conform first to library needs and services; only a competent librarian can determine these matters. The architect should be required to make his plans conform to the librarian's specifications and adapt the architectural design to the requirements of the building. A beautiful building in a central location should house the library, but the efficient distribution of the books to readers is the major requirement.

The library has a strong appeal to many people, and it is one of the causes for which funds can be raised rather easily. Princeton has developed this appeal by designating donors to the library as "Friends of Princeton Library" and this recognition has been appreciated.

It is the responsibility of the trustees to fix a policy for as generous support of the library as possible; to see that it is administered ably and efficiently, and to assure themselves that the library, its books, and services are suitable for the institution's needs.

CHAPTER 13

DAILY CHAPEL

NEXT to the library, without which a college cannot exist, daily chapel can be the most powerful center of influence on a college campus. Daily chapel has been a very significant part of the life of most American colleges and universities. It can be so still, where the enrollment is not too large. Where the college enrolls few enough students so they can all assemble together in the chapel available, great values are conserved through required daily attendance.

The position of president was formerly held almost exclusively by clergymen. To them chapel was a very natural and essential service. Clergymen are less frequently appointed now, and many presidents recruited from the laity have failed to grasp the value of chapel as a spiritual and social influence, and as an institutional center about which the very diversified life of the modern college can revolve.

It is a great thing for all the students to assemble together daily, to meet each other on the way to and from chapel, and to sit together by classes. It is a great thing for the president to preside, to read a portion of Scripture, and lead this great group of students in prayer and for all to join in a familiar hymn. It is a great thing for the president to be able to address briefly the entire student body on any matter of common concern, to see them all daily, and to be seen by them.

It is difficult to sum it up in a convincing way, but as one who attended compulsory daily chapel, and who presided at chapel for sixteen years, the writer is glad to register his faith in it as a college institution.

College chapel is a religious service. It cannot be maintained on the basis of being instructive. It is and always was a simple assembly of students and faculty in a brief, formal religious service. Where an attempt has been made to turn it over to the students, to bring in interesting speakers, to make it a musical entertainment or otherwise distort its religious character, the result has almost invariably been the abandonment of chapel.

In many instances the student body outgrew any available assembly hall, and required chapel had to be given up. College chapel is a rather intimate service and loses its values where thousands hear through loud speakers.

Where it is continued as a voluntary service, it may well be worth while, but a very definite part of its strength lies somehow in all students assembling by classes and in the consciousness that each feels himself to be a part of the whole college.

In many institutions, required daily chapel is definitely a thing of the past, and it cannot be revived. Where the college is still small and where it is still required, it should be cherished as one of the most important and precious academic functions.

CHAPTER 14

SCHOLARSHIP AND STUDENT ACTIVITIES

WHILE the whole institution is maintained for the students and, therefore, everything relates to them, there are some matters peculiarly the students' which concern trustees.

Scholarship

There is much talk around every college, and it is sometimes heard from trustees, to the effect that good grades are unimportant, mean little; that student activities, athletics, and fraternities are the more important in the student's life. This is exactly the same as saying to an employee of any large industry, that how he does his work is unimportant; that the important thing to him is to play good golf, be active socially, and belong to the right club. Mastering their studies is the job of college students, and such mastery earns high grades. When this is done student activities are a grand recreation, but they are no more the real job than good golf is the main job for an employee in industry.

Trustees should be very clear about this. If their institution is to be of value as a college or university, it must stand squarely for high scholarship and for the high character which leads students to do their work to the best of their ability. All of this is the business and responsibility of the faculty, and they can usually be relied upon to cherish scholarly ability and maintain standards. It does help enormously, however, if the trustees appreciate scholarship and high intellectual attainment in the students, and give their full support to keeping first things first, and athletics and student activities in their proper place.

[125]

There is ample evidence that the students who rank among the highest 10 per cent in their classes in scholarship send more men on to distinguished success than any other 10 per cent of their classmates and often more than the remaining 90 per cent. Of course, many succeed who do not make high grades, but the percentage who succeed is far higher among those who do their college work with distinction.

In an extensive study of students' grades it is surprising to find that most students pursue throughout their course a certain level of attainment. Usually the student remains excellent, average, or inferior all through his four years. Also, those who are excellent in high school are usually excellent in college. By the same token, those who have the ability, persistence, and sense of duty to lead them to do excellent work in high school and college usually do equally well whatever they attempt on leaving college. Success in football, unsupported by high grades, is more likely to lead to success in professional football than to success in law, medicine, or business.

Student Activities

While success in scholarly attainment comes first, student contacts and student activities do come second among the educational agencies of the college. Much is learned of life and men on the play field and in student discussion of student affairs.

Here each student can show his own initiative; can compete in a field of his own choosing with his classmates. Student activities belong to the students and can be left largely in the students' hands. It is the responsibility of the institution to know that its student affairs are wholesome, fairly run, and are a credit to the institution.

College Publications

It is most undesirable to censor the student publications. In the opinion of the writer, the administration should insure the selection of editors who are honest, capable students of good judgment, and then leave the editing to them. If an irresponsible, fanatical, or wildly radical student is made editor, he can do the college much harm and be a constant source of irritation to administration, faculty, and alumni without accomplishing any good. It seems wise and reasonable to have a professor or committee pass on nominations for the editorship sufficiently to insure that only men and women are nominated who are capable and of such stability of character as to be worthy to represent the college in this capacity.

Auditing Accounts of Student Activities

While it is desirable that students manage their own affairs, the institution does have a real responsibility for the integrity of all money transactions. Otherwise, many students will develop ideas and habits of graft and loose business methods greatly to their injury. Probably most colleges of 500 students have 50 student organizations, and the larger institutions usually maintain well over 200. Each has a student treasurer, business manager, or steward who should keep careful and intelligible accounts. However, they are not usually appointed or elected on account of their business ability or their knowledge of business methods, but rather because of their popularity with their group.

Anyone who has had occasion to attempt to audit accounts kept by unsupervised students has certainly been surprised at the number of different mistakes that can be made and the amount of neglect that can develop. The total funds thus handled annually by students, including fraternity, sorority, and boarding club funds, can easily amount to several hundred thousand dollars in any large institution.

Certainly it devolves on the administration to see that this money is handled honestly, free from any graft, and that exact and complete accounts are rendered. This can be done only through a competent, patient, and sympathetic auditor of student activities, who provides or approves accounting forms, systems, and procedures, and whose approval each student financial officer must secure.

While the installation of such a system usually meets with opposition, after it is installed its services are very generally appreciated. A student rarely wants to be a grafter, to end his term with a deficit, or to turn over to his successor faulty accounts. The trouble is that usually he has no experience in business matters and finds bookkeeping and collecting rather a bore. With suitable books provided and some directions, and with the necessity of having his accounts audited at frequent intervals, he finds satisfaction in correct work.

In an institution where such a system of auditing student activity accounts has been in effect a few years, deficits become exceptional, and most organizations operate with a surplus.

Where this system is carried out with the largest control, all money is deposited in a student activity account with the college treasurer, and all checks are countersigned by some one in the college office who knows that the organization has a balance to cover the check.

The effect of such a system has great educational value. Each treasurer learns how to keep a good set of books accurately. He or she becomes accustomed to sound business methods. The idea that any one can use public funds for private purposes, and the word "graft" are banished from the campus.

Financial Aid to Students

As it is the ambition of every institution to enroll as many able students as possible, and as most of the ablest students come from families of limited means, practically every college and university helps finance the education of promising students who need assistance. Ordinarily, this financial assistance is given in four different ways:

1. *Scholarships* won by high intellectual attainment. These may be presented to students who have made a high record in the secondary school, or they may be granted as a result of competitive examinations. In all cases, they are a recognition of high scholarly attainment, and in the great majority of cases are equivalent to a part or all the tuition charged. Stated another way scholarships are a reduction of tuition to students of high promise.

2. *Grants in Aid* differ from scholarships in that they are given to assist needy students, but are not a reward for high scholarship. While they are rarely given to students with inferior records, they are usually given to needy students of average ability, who promise to make a creditable, but not a brilliant college record.

3. *Loans.* It is increasingly the practice to maintain funds from which loans are made to needy students with good college records. Usually the loans are only available to upper class students who are well known as to their college work and trustworthiness. These loans are rarely in excess of $200 or $250 a year, with a limit of $400 to $800 loaned to any one student. The interest rate while in college varies from nothing to 6 per cent. Such loans are usually repaid in monthly installments of $10 or some multiple of $5, and these loans are generally repaid promptly.

Where every reasonable precaution is taken to select trustworthy students, and where collection is carefully followed up, nearly all loans are repaid. At one institution now loaning $50,000 annually, a student in order to secure a loan must have a general average in scholarship slightly above that required for graduation; he must have three men who know him well vouch for his honesty; and he must take out $500 life insurance and assign it to the Loan Fund as security in

case of death. At that institution the total losses since loans
began in 1912 have amounted to only $3,000.

4. *Employment.* Every institution employs a considerable
number of students in various kinds of work: janitor work,
assistance in the library, care of grounds, assisting in laboratories, stenographic work, waiting tables, etc. Under the
depression's National Youth Administration, an astonishing
amount of work was found for college students. The work was
usually paid for at from 50 cents to $1.25 per hour, the pre-
vailing rate being about 75 cents.

In addition to work on the campus, more or less work for
students is always available in the town. National studies
have shown that about 60 per cent of all college students must
have financial help of some kind to attend college.

In spite of all that is being done to aid worthy and capable
students, many thousands who would greatly profit from
college training are still excluded by lack of money. Also
many able students, in struggling to support themselves in
college, are overworking, and are forced by many hours of
labor to do an inferior grade of college work. Much remains
to be done, both in excluding those of inferior ability from
college and university, and in financing the proper education
of those who are fully able to profit but lack resources.

Student Health Service

In recent years colleges have become conscious of their
responsibilities relative to the health of their students. Nearly
all colleges have some formally organized health service.
This ranges from the part-time services of a local doctor to a
complete hospital of 50 to 100 beds, with a staff of doctors,
nurses, and technicians.

The usual services consist of a physical examination by the
college physician on entrance, with such periodic or special
follow-up examinations as seem desirable. A daily clinic is

usually held, and treatment is provided for injuries on the athletic field. Where there is a good city hospital with adequate facilities, it is usual to have an arrangement by which students can be cared for there in case of sickness, and for surgical operations.

If the college maintains its own hospital and staff, morning and afternoon clinics take care of minor matters, and students needing hospitalization are cared for. All except very minor surgery is either sent out to a hospital with a surgical staff, or if an operating room is provided, expert surgeons are called in when required.

Usually with a student body of 1,000 or more, a $7 to $10 hospital fee with such charges as are necessarily assessed, meet the expense. The fee covers all needed physical examination, free clinical service, and usually two to four days free in the hospital. Medicine, X-rays, and unusual expenses are paid for by students at cost. Faculty members or others than students served usually pay reasonable fees for all services.

A college hospital with an adequate staff serves several uses. It enables the institution to insure prompt and economical service to all ailing students. It largely relieves parents of anxiety lest their child should be neglected when sick. It greatly reduces the incidence of contagious diseases, many of which are brought to the campus by students. It encourages dormitory directors and fraternity members to insist on sick students going to the hospital promptly. Finally, and by no means least in importance, is the familiarizing of all students with a good hospital and a competent medical and nursing staff and their education in what such an institution can do for them.

CHAPTER 15

INTERCOLLEGIATE ATHLETICS

PROBABLY in no other phase of the college or university are things both so well and so poorly done. The instruction and training of the major athletic teams is likely to be the best, the most individual, and the most expensive teaching done on the campus.

Regardless of the size of the institution, its major intercollegiate teams involve about 200 men. Each man is very carefully selected for his special fitness for the team and the position on the team in which he will play. He is given individual coaching and supervised practice in his special field, and plays eight to twenty intercollegiate games under the critical eye of his teacher. His diet, sleep, and all habits bearing on his health are carefully watched. Very often this superb training and experience in good sportsmanship contribute largely to the personality and later success of the student.

But no matter how many thousand men the institution may enroll, only about 200 receive this superb training, and usually the fine training of the 200 is done very largely at the expense of all the others. Of these 200 men some 40 in football bring yearly income of from a few thousand to $500,-000 or more, the amount depending largely on their team's success.

Intercollegiate athletics are an excellent thing for the most brilliant athletes on the campus in that they have the opportunity to meet their equals or superiors from other campuses. So far as they involve large gate receipts, intercollegiate athletics are undesirable. They put the emphasis far too strongly on winning, as winning teams attract the largest gate receipts, and they bring great pressure on the alumni, the coaches, the athletic director, and on the college administration to hire brilliant athletes.

As intercollegiate athletics are now handled it is difficult to fix a policy which is wholly good. Almost all who officiate at games today are capable and fearless, and intercollegiate athletics are quite free from unfair practice or play dangerous for well-trained men. The games themselves are not usually open to much criticism. The rule prohibiting the playing of a freshman or a first-year transfer has reduced the hiring of players somewhat. Scholarship rules, where rigidly enforced, put a further check on hiring players. In spite of all this it is very difficult to be certain that every player on a team is a real college student, on his way to graduation, who came to college for an education and not to play football. The fact that everyone knows that a winning team takes in many thousand dollars more than a losing team greatly increases the pressure to secure able players at any price and also provides the money for securing the players unless receipts are closely guarded by careful auditing.

Another serious objection to present-day intercollegiate athletics lies in the tremendous claim it makes on the time and vigor of the men on the teams. Strenuous practice for several hours almost every day during the season, usually classes at night on strategy and rules, with one or two major games each week, with the travel and time away from college involved, all make it extremely difficult for the student to maintain his scholarship. Add to this that most players are inevitably poor boys and must be dependent on some means of earning a part or all their expenses, and you have another reason for subsidizing players.

Massachusetts Institute of Technology does not play intercollegiate football. Chicago withdrew from her conference competition and now plays only such sports and such teams as she elects. Swarthmore has an athletic system including all students and plays several football teams without great concern for gate receipts. Unless some concessions are allowed major athletes in financial aids, nominal work, easy scholarship requirements, or in other ways, it is rarely possible to maintain a team that can win half its games with institutions of equal class and equal enrollment.

The trustees and the administration are clearly faced with three alternatives: 1. To give various concessions to a certain number of major athletes. This will include financial aid directly or indirectly. 2. Accepting willingly the inability of the team to win half its games with institutions of its class. 3. Give up intercollegiate athletics in football altogether or at least in the conference in which the institution would normally play and with this the hope of any considerable gate receipts, and play teams in the class with the team maintained.

There are a few definite recommendations that can be made with confidence. The athletic department and all coaches should be an integral part of the Department of Physical Education, under the complete control and direction of the head of that department. All athletic income and expense should pass through the hands of the college business office and be audited there, subject to all the usual rules of the institution. The head football coach should not be paid more than a full professor. Cases are on record where the coach was paid more than the president. Indebtedness should not be incurred for a stadium, fieldhouse, or other capital investment in excess of a conservative estimate of the net income from athletics for two or at most three years. Otherwise, the institution sells out its control of its coaching staff and its team to those who made the loan.

Intercollegiate athletics have so much good in them and yet involve so many problems, difficulties, and temptations, that it will be long before a fully satisfactory system for America is evolved.

CHAPTER 16

FRATERNITIES AND SORORITIES

THESE organizations are found in a great many colleges and universities. In many places in the past they have been the cause of serious problems of various kinds. In more recent years, through the efforts of their national secretaries, they have been managed better and much more in harmony with college administrations.

Essentially, these organizations are clubs, the active members electing all new members, the chief object being to promote the social life of the members and, with few exceptions, to operate a clubhouse providing rooms and board for all or part of the members. While they stress the fact that they are secret societies, they differ very little in plan of organization and operation from the men's clubs with restricted membership found in all large cities.

It costs about $100 a year more for a member to pay his dues and live in a fraternity house than for a nonmember to live modestly outside. Usually the living quarters are pleasant, and the food served is good. Membership usually ranges from thirty-five to ninety, with some smaller and some larger chapters. The social life is pleasant and generally wholesome. The tendency of most fraternities is toward overemphasis on social life and participation in student activities, and away from high scholarship.

On the whole the members and alumni under national supervision can be depended upon for the successful operation of these houses. There are, however, a few points on which control and assistance can well be given locally. Especially, an institution can be truly helpful in auditing fraternity accounts, providing some common social control, and in keeping a check on the scholarship of fraternity members.

Auditing Fraternity Accounts

An organization of thirty members providing rooms and board will handle $9,000 or more a year. In many fraternities with large membership, this may run to $20,000 or more. This is too large a sum to be handled by inexperienced undergraduates without careful supervision. Where no supervision is given, usually one-third of the organizations on a campus are poorly managed each year, collections run behind, and expense exceeds income. Where such poor management exists its influence on the members of the organization encourages carelessness in money affairs.

Today many institutions provide in connection with the business office an auditor of fraternity and sorority accounts, or have them audited by the auditor of student activities. Suitable books and forms are required, generally uniform throughout all organizations, and they are audited monthly. Under such supervision, collections are made promptly, deficits are rare, the treasurer receives excellent business training, and the whole business tone of the organization is good. Usually a charge of 1 or 2 per cent of the gross receipts is made to cover cost, so that the audit is entirely self-supporting. As each fraternity must prepare a budget and operate within its receipts, extravagant parties are avoided, and useless competition among organizations in expensive ways is effectively discouraged.

Social Control

On the whole the aims of the social organization and of the administration are the same. Both desire parties to be pleasant and respectable. Both wish to avoid anything bordering on scandal. Almost always when undesirable happenings occur, it is due to ignorance of good social practice on the part of those responsible, to undesirable leadership in the social committee, or to excesses of uncontrolled alumni.

Today most fraternities and all sororities maintain a resident housemother. Usually she is able to maintain the social life and all parties on a pleasant and satisfactory level. It is advantageous for the institution to pay part of the housemother's salary, as this insures a reasonable wage, gives the proper official of the institution a part in selecting desirable persons for these positions, and makes the housemother directly responsible to the institution. Twenty dollars a month is paid fraternity house mothers by one college and this seems adequate to promote a wholesome relationship.

In a large institution it is worthwhile to employ a competent woman of attractive personality to work with all students responsible for the management of college social affairs inside and outside the fraternities. The assistance such a person gives can not only greatly aid the students in making their affairs pleasant and agreeable, but it enables the institution to keep sufficient touch and control to avoid most undesirable parties. The American college in the end is responsible for the character of the social life of its students.

The old theory that the college president stands in the place of the parents to all students is rather appalling when there are thousands of students, but it is hard to reach any other conclusion in regard to this relationship. The parents do look to the college, and therefore to the president, as responsible for the care of their children's health, morals, and social conduct. The college should make certain that fraternity and sorority parties are pleasant, properly conducted, and such as the parents could approve.

Further, the students attending American colleges constitute one of the most heterogeneous groups imaginable so far as social background is concerned. Many young people very promising in ability are almost wholly lacking in any social experience. A very great service is rendered them, if while in college they form correct ideals of social life and have some experience in conducting themselves properly at social affairs. We are constantly graduating from every institution students who, while coming from very simple, humble homes, have outstanding ability. At college they should not only be trained to serve largely, but should there develop the social grace to enable them to serve in high places with becoming manners.

Scholarship

It is reasonable and desirable to encourage fraternity members to elect as president and other important officers in the organization, members of good scholarly standing. A good attitude toward scholarly work cannot be expected of a society whose leaders rank below, or just at the minimum average required for graduation. It is always to be remembered that these societies have real pride in their organizations and do not intentionally elect unworthy students to office. Some advice and encouragement along this line rather than rules will generally be effective.

In institutions with low entrance requirements, such as mere high school graduation, pledging and initiation, or at least initiation, should be limited by college rules to students who give evidence of their ability to carry on their college course to graduation. If an organization is allowed to bring into its membership a considerable proportion of students indifferent to scholarship, its influence on new members must be bad. For an institution to cherish a society with special privileges, claiming superior social standing, which is made up of members and led by officers indifferent or opposed to high scholarship, is certainly both absurd and unwise.

With financial control and some social direction, it is

possible to develop the fraternities and sororities into very useful organizations, contributing a considerable value to the institutional life and doing much to develop fine social ideals in their members.

CHAPTER 17

COLLEGE RESIDENCE HALLS

THE trustees of every institution should have a well-defined policy as to what dormitories they desire ultimately to build. Their location is important, and ground must be reserved for them or purchased. Dormitories for men and women should each have natural preferential sites. The whole problem will be much simplified and clarified if the trustees can reach a conclusion as to what is ultimately desirable.

If this first question is settled to the effect that dormitories are to be ultimately provided, the second question is the style of architecture and their cost. Dormitories have been built of relatively fire-proof construction ranging all the way from $500 to $15,000 per student housed, and some general limit on cost per student goes far to determine their architectural style and limitations. Certainly, the style of architecture should harmonize with the general style of architecture of the other buildings.

The cost will be determined by various factors. Perhaps most important is the quality of housing desirable for the type of students the institution expects to serve. Simple, crowded quarters might not attract students from families of ample means, while elaborate, expensive quarters certainly would not be suitable for students coming from low-income families. Assuming the land is available, that the dining room facilities are included in the building, and that most students are housed two in a room with common bath rooms in each corridor, the lowest practical cost will range from $2,000 to $3,000 per student.

[140]

Probably the most expensive dormitory that could be justified in a publicly supported institution would range in cost from $3,500 to $4,500 per student housed. Above this figure material increase in space per student, architectural beauty, and other luxuries enter into the costs. They can go to almost any figure.

In determining the rental charge, some consideration must be given to the prevailing room rent in the city in the vicinity of the college. The lowest room rent generally charged is $100 for the college year. This is about $3.00 a week per student. It is exceptional for rooms to exceed $300 or $350 per student for the college year.

The cost of operating the dormitory, including supervision, service, light, heat and water, and repairs to furniture and building, can be kept down to about $120 per student, if the students take care of their rooms. With complete care of room provided, it may run to $125 to $175 per student.

The room rent charged should certainly be ample to pay all costs of operation and maintenance, and 4 per cent on the total dormitory investment. Housing and boarding students is purely personal service and should not be provided below cost. If it is desired to reduce the cost to students below cost and reasonable interest, it should be done by grants-in-aid to needy students, and not in reduction of room rent.

It is rarely economical to house fewer than 100 students in one dormitory unit, although perhaps the ideal social unit would be 60 to 80. On the other hand, probably 200 or 300 is as large a group as can be conveniently cared for in one building. From 125 to 150 seems to be the best number if economy of operation and the best interests of the students are both regarded.

Great profit in planning dormitories will result from visits to institutions providing dormitories of the general character contemplated. Harvard and Yale perhaps have the most generous dormitory provision. Dartmouth houses all students in dormitories and has invested a considerable portion of her endowment in dormitories. Most of the important women's colleges throughout the country house their students in dormitories. Miami University at Oxford, Ohio, University of Illinois, University of Minnesota, Iowa State College, University of Iowa, Iowa State Teachers College are of interest as representing public institutions which now house a large percentage of their students in dormitories. It is rapidly being accepted as sound policy to house all students in dormitories, or in dormitories and fraternity and club houses. Most of our older, privately supported institutions have endeavored to provide ample dormitories for many years. The movement among publicly supported institutions has by no means kept pace with the increasing enrollment of students.

Building Dormitories With Dormitory Income

A number of state institutions are authorized to make loans secured by dormitory net income for the building of additional dormitories. With sufficient dormitories in operation to produce a minimum net income of a few thousand or more, this is a satisfactory plan. The more net income the quicker the loan can be retired. In some cases bonds secured by dormitory net income are sold; in other cases the money is borrowed from a bank on notes. Over the years all dormitories desired can be financed under this plan.

CHAPTER 18

PLACEMENT OF GRADUATES IN EMPLOYMENT, AND ALUMNI RELATIONS

A GREAT variation in policy prevails among colleges and universities relative to the placement in employment of their graduates. While some institutions concern themselves very little in this matter and disclaim responsibility, others feel responsible for the employment of every graduate.

It would seem that an institution which encouraged young people to spend four years under its care and instruction "as a preparation for life" would be much concerned to see that they met with maximum success in life, and that it would do everything possible to give them a good start.

The lack of concern common among colleges probably is a survival of the sentiment developed many years ago when practically all college graduates were preparing to enter theological schools, and later to enter theology or other professions. Such students' future plans were clear and definite, and they needed no placement assistance. Later, when a considerable number of graduates began to enter other occupations outside the professions, most college students came from families of the well-to-do, and the graduate's father or other relatives were quite able to look after his employment.

Today this whole situation is changed. While perhaps one-third to one-half of the 250,000 who graduate annually from colleges and universities need no assistance in placement, the rest need help very much. A much smaller proportion than formerly enter the professions. When these complete their professional training, assistance in getting established in professional employment is very often badly needed, as was not the case in the past. Also today a large proportion of our college graduates, and many of our ablest, come from lower middle-class families, lacking experience or familiarity with the fields of employment of their sons and daughters, and having no useful personal contacts with these fields. Often, in fact generally, the young graduate has prepared to enter employment in a field entirely outside his own or his family's acquaintance. It is now enormously helpful to the average college graduate to be placed in employment through the assistance of his alma mater.

On the other hand, employers are forced to turn to the colleges and universities for help in securing the graduates they desire to employ. The personnel or employment office of the institution is more and more required to act as middleman between the employer and the graduate—the agency which brings the right employer and the right graduate together. Such a department through the years establishes a great many contacts with business, industry, professional and graduate schools, employers of teachers, etc., so that each year many calls for graduates come in from old friends.

Finally, the satisfactory placement of its graduates is good policy for any school. Probably the actual outlay of the college on each graduate ranges from $1,200 for a four-year college graduate to as high as $10,000 or over in the case of students who spend eight years in undergraduate and professional schools at our greater universities. If this expenditure was really made with the purpose of fitting the graduate for effective living and service, it would seem that the least the institution could do would be to place her graduates' feet on the ladder of employment and service.

Also the real test of the value of college training in any field is the ability of the graduate to live wisely and serve usefully in the world in the field of his preparation. Every institution should be constantly seeking to test the skill of its teachers, the suitability of its courses, and the value of its training, by noting the ease or difficulty with which it places its graduates in appropriate positions, and the success these graduates achieve.

One other aspect of the work of an institution relative to placement of graduates should be noted. It is important not to train more in a specific field than can be employed. Where narrowly directed training is given, as in mining engineering, or veterinary medicine, or in training for the doctorate in English, or history, or German, it is undesirable to graduate more than can be placed in employment in the field of their training at a reasonably satisfactory salary. An annual report in the fall covering placement in each field will indicate where too many or too few are being trained. The tendency of each department and each college is to magnify its own work, to seek continually larger numbers, to rejoice at an increased number of graduates. This enthusiasm is often tempered if they are definitely expected to place their graduates in positions.

If a college has unreasonable difficulty in placing its graduates, this fact raises a question as to whether its courses are organized as they should be or whether their graduates have been well trained. In such a case the trustees might ask the president to look into the matter thoroughly and suggest what procedure might improve the situation.

The most common causes of failure to place graduates, chargeable to the institution, are as follows:

1. Ineffective placement office.

2. Students of low ability or of very inferior personality have been inadvisedly graduated from courses offering employment only to capable persons.

3. More students are graduated from a given course than there are openings for employment.

4. The curricula offered are not suitable for the employment opportunities available.

Alumni Relations

For many years the older private institutions have had their alumni well organized, chiefly with a view to securing alumni financial support. More recently many public institutions have developed effective organizations of their alumni. Today practically every college, as well as every university, has an active alumni organization. Alumni over the country have contributed a great deal of money to their alma maters. Until quite recently alumni secretaries were chiefly occupied in maintaining a directory of the alumni, publishing an alumni journal, and soliciting the alumni for contributions. But lately there has been a marked shift toward serving the alumni. This has taken several directions. One has been to organize courses for alumni at the Commencement season. Another has been to endeavor to suggest current reading for alumni. Most important has been the effort to make the alumni feel that the alumni secretary is their representative at the college—the secretary *for* the alumni—who is there to serve them in any way they may desire his services. There are many services of great variety which the alumni, particularly the younger alumni, may desire from their alma mater. The alumni secretary has easy access to all the administrative and departmental offices. He can be the ideal avenue of access for the alumni to needed aid from the institution. The alumni secretary can talk over the employment prospects of an alumnus with the placement officer. He can obtain needed information for an alumnus from a department or place him in contact with the right man in the department. He can look up records in the registrar's office. The college personnel and organization changes, and after a few years an alumnus is often quite out of touch even with his own department, and a secretary for the alumni can be most useful.

It seems possible as time passes that the function of the alumni secretary will shift entirely away from soliciting funds. This activity may be transferred to the business office, or placed in the hands of an able man associated with the alumni secretary, but distinct from him. The secretary for the alumni may devote all his efforts to extending the services of the institution to the alumni, in editing the alumni journal, in maintaining the alumni directory, in serving as the agent of the alumni at the institution, in aiding alumni to secure better positions where needed. It seems highly probable that alumni will look more and more to their alma mater. Happily, the encouragement of this continuing relation will undoubtedly increase the gifts of alumni.

Recently a few of our great state universities have carried on well-organized campaigns to raise funds from alumni, with more than usual success. Each graduate has received a free gift from the state in education costing from $1,200 to $5,000 beyond all fees paid, the latter figure in the case of those who complete courses in professional schools. These alumni should recognize an obligation to the state in this amount. It can be paid in large and generous service and in many cases can only be repaid in this way. But every alumnus who is able should realize this obligation and repay it in cash if he can, in whole or in part.

There has been a widespread feeling that our alumni owe nothing to a state-supported institution, other than to pay the ordinary taxes from which it is supported. This narrow view is changing. To a considerable degree the excellence of service of any institution, private or public, can be gauged by the recognition by the alumni of their financial debt to their alma mater.

Far too often the alumni interest centers chiefly on their alma mater's success in athletics, especially in football. The intensity of the demand for winning football teams has decreased somewhat in the last twenty-five years, and there are increasing numbers of institutions with very loyal and enthusiastic alumni where athletic competition, and especially in football, is relatively unimportant. The University of Chicago, Massachusetts Institute of Technology, California Institute of Technology, Swarthmore, Haverford, Rochester, and Johns Hopkins might be mentioned as examples. At many other institutions, such as Harvard, Princeton, Iowa State College, or the University of North Carolina, other aspects of the work and life of the institutions absorb relatively a much larger proportion of alumni attention than formerly.

The trustees can well concern themselves that the institution under their direction maintains a cordial and wholesome relation with its alumni, that a continual effort is made to keep the alumni well informed and broadly interested.

SECTION IV

The Need for Looking Ahead

EACH INSTITUTION SHOULD SEEK ITS OWN PROPER LEVEL

THE time has gone when just *any* college may hope to become great. There was a time when colleges in America were few, when the pattern of the ultimate development of the country was unknown, when any founder might reasonably hope that his college would grow to become an institution of great distinction.

Today, with 1,880 colleges, universities, and technical institutes in operation, much is settled. For certain professional fields there is ample provision. In certain areas there are many colleges. Each institution is largely limited by its location, the development of adjacent institutions, and by its financial resources.

Toward what level of service is your college headed? What may it best aim to do 25 years, 50 years, 100 years hence? What can it best do to supplement the services of the other institutions in its area? Try to view the future of your college in terms of the moving and dynamic future of American education as a whole.

All of your present planning will take clearer shape if the ultimate level of work and service of your college is agreed upon. A list of the various commonly recognized types of institutions may be of use in thinking of your institution.

Junior Colleges (Two Years)

1. Offering courses to fit students for entering the junior year of a four-year college or university.

2. Offering vocational terminal courses designed to carry

students one or two years beyond high school and give them vocational training in secretarial work, auto mechanics, salesmanship, or other subjects that will fit them to enter an occupation well prepared.

3. Offering both 1 and 2.

Colleges of Arts and Sciences (Four Years)

1. Limited to liberal arts and sciences.

2. Liberal arts and sciences with some vocational courses. The most frequently met vocational course is education, preparing teachers for high schools. Courses in commerce and engineering, journalism, and other subjects are also found. If vocational courses are offered they should be honestly supported and taught in a manner worthy of the institution, and not merely used as advertising devices for purposes of competition.

3. Either of the above with graduate work for the masters degree added. If graduate work is offered, it should be carefully limited to fields adequately staffed with professors able to direct worthwhile graduate work at a level comparable with that given at the universities for the same degree.

Technical Institutes, Offering Technical, Vocational Courses Only

1. Undergraduate only. The fields of instruction should be sharply determined.

2. Undergraduate and graduate. The fields of undergraduate instruction should be carefully determined and fixed. The scope and purpose of graduate work and research should be carefully fixed within the important fields of instruction and within the financial capacity of the institution.

University

Determine clearly the undergraduate vocational and professional fields in which instruction will be given. Determine fields of graduate work and research, limiting them sharply to the fields peculiarly suitable and necessary to the institution and within her financial ability, and support these fields generously. A few fields well developed and supported are far better than many fields inadequately supported.

After the level of an institution is settled it should be developed at this level with several governing ideas prominently in mind.

1. Every institution has a personality of its own. Preserve it and do not violate it.

2. Preserve the integrity of the institution. Take no action that may seem to reflect unfavorably on the institutional integrity, honesty, and sincerity.

3. Stop thinking in terms of competition with other neighboring institutions. Think of how best you can cooperate with them. The work of education, like that of religion, will never be so completely accomplished that energy can be spared for competition.

There are now developing numerous fields in which cooperation is being effected. In some cases colleges are cooperating in instruction, library development, and in other ways with nearby institutions. Swarthmore, the University of Pennsylvania, Haverford, and Bryn Mawr have developed cooperative enterprises in research, teaching, and use of facilities that point to a rich and significant program in the future. Among university and college libraries cooperation has already become an important aspect of the educational picture. Efforts are made to avoid unnecessarily duplicating expensive collections; also by lending freely and by use of microfilms, the unnecessary purchase of expensive books is avoided.

A notable instance of cooperation is that between the University of Texas and the University of Chicago in operating together a great astronomical observatory in Texas.

Does the education offered by your college best suit the needs of your constituents?

Education is very conservative. Times and constituents change; what was most suitable once may not be suitable now. Yet a faculty tends to perpetuate courses and curricula as they were, without much change, and with few new departures.

Present offerings are not necessarily the best that could be given. Often a college can materially improve its services to its students without material increase in expense. Any such change usually must originate with the trustees or the administration.

Test the education given by your college against the educational needs of your constituents. While the great majority of educational needs are probably identical with those of other constituencies there may be one or more peculiar, outstanding need here. If so, are you serving it?

Does your institution draw her students chiefly from:

1. A very limited geographical area?
2. A special constituency, as members of a certain religious sect?
3. A region where a single industry is dominant?
4. From one of the distinct regions of the United States?
5. From all over the nation?

After the origin of the major part of the students is determined, endeavor to determine whether the offerings of the institution are those which will best serve these students. Should the appeal of the college best be carefully restricted or widely extended. If there are some special needs, serve them. If there are only standard needs, why attempt to cover everything?

A few illustrations may be useful. At Akron, the great rubber center of the country, the University of Akron offers strong courses in the chemistry of rubber. Alfred University, located near great ceramic industries, maintains one of the strong departments of ceramics. The Agricultural and Mechanical College of Texas and Iowa State College, each in the center of great livestock areas, maintain strong veterinary colleges.

So far as possible, develop to its highest the particular potential strength of your institution, rather than dissipate her finances in an attempt to compete with every rival.

CHAPTER 20

COMMON AIMS AND GOALS

AN administration to fully serve an institution, must not only deal effectively with such matters as have been discussed previously, but it must also develop the educational statesmanship to plan for the future on the highest level. College administration is not a thing in itself but a means to an end. To be distinguished it must have clear aims in what it intends to do for each student; also it must be conscious of the relations of administrative decisions to the larger aims of the college. To illustrate the latter point, note that the decision on a minor matter, in its form and in the way it is reached, may be destructive to the democratic spirit of the college. Some modification of the statement of the decision or of procedure might have attained the same end without any adverse effect on larger values.

To do effective job planning on a high level for an institution, the following questions must be faced:

1. What are the common aims of American education, and how far is your institution pursuing these several aims?

2. Has your institution found its own proper level in American education?

3. Are the types of education offered by your institution the types needed by your constituents?

4. How effectively is your institution serving each individual student?

Common Aims or Goals

While institutions of higher learning differ greatly one from another, there are a number of aims or goals common to all.

They are pursued with different degrees of zeal. In one institution vocational goals are most emphasized, while cultural goals are of greatest concern in others.

It is important to determine which of these aims your institution should emphasize and whether it is pursuing all the important aims that it should. Nearly every administrative policy has a bearing, directly or indirectly, on the effectiveness with which one or another of these aims is attained. For example, the policy relative to the maintenance of fraternity houses and dormitories bears directly on the social development of the students. The policy relative to the quality of students admitted materially affects the quality and level of the teaching, and of the professional excellence of graduates.

The following may be considered some of the more important common aims of higher education:

Cultural. We all share in the heritage and tradition of thought, which it is undoubtedly a prime duty of our universities and colleges to preserve, interpret, pass on to the next generation, and enlarge. In a broad way most of the work of a college is directed to this end. However, in this day of specialization and minute scholarship, these large responsibilities are often lost sight of in the pursuit of detail. Is your college administration intent on this large duty?

1. Is your college so organized and motivated as to enable it to recognize students and staff members of peculiar ability and develop their strength?

Our nation needs leaders who can pioneer in every field of creative thought, in every branch of science; critics and interpreters of our national life; men who can synthesize the progress and thinking of America and point it onward and upward. Men who have such capacities are rare, but one may enter your college as a freshman this year. He may not conform to the usual average standards. It may require special insight to see promise in him. If such a man entered your college, would he be identified and developed along the line of his strength, or would he be forced into the mold of the average student? Is your college intent on developing the very able, or is it leaving the discovery and development of such men to Harvard and Chicago?

Some college freshmen, while having great gifts and large possibilities, have small taste for and show little promise in the regular courses. What chance is there that such a one will be recognized, and challenged by suitable work at your college, and not dropped out as an unpromising student?

Our most outstanding example of a great man who was a dull and unsatisfactory student from the elementary school through college is Winston Churchill. Formal schooling did not touch him. It was not until he entered the Army in India and began to read widely on his own initiative, that he awoke to serious interests beyond polo. Many other notable instances could be cited where the routine of college, well suited to the average, has failed entirely to recognize or serve the unusual. Is your college on the alert to serve the unusual student?

2. There are certain qualities widely regarded as indicating an educated gentleman—qualities of character, culture, and courtesy. Knowledge in itself seems sterile and barren unless supported by character.

What is your institution doing to give knowledge of, and experience in courtesy and gentleness in living with others?

Does it give each student some knowledge and appreciation of great literature?

Of great art?

Of great music?

Does it give each student some introduction to the fields of knowledge outside the general area of his specialization?

Are the graduates of your college men and women who are easy to live with and pleasant to talk with?

Vocational. Our first American colleges were established to train men for the ministry. They all started with a definite vocational purpose. If the roll of the college graduates of 1700–1800 is examined, it will be seen that practically all entered the ministry or the law, with a few entering teaching and medicine. Whatever else a college may do, it always carries a definite vocational responsibility for its students. We like to say today that if we train the student to think he will be prepared for any vocation. While ability to think is vital, a student expects to gain much more in college toward fitting him for a vocation.

Unfortunately, many college teachers have come to regard any type of vocational training as improper and undignified. This is scarcely a productive attitude. Certainly give all the culture and breadth of training and practice in correct thinking to students that is possible, but also prepare them, so far as possible, for their life work.

What is your college doing to prepare its students to earn a living? This can best be considered by stating the different forms vocational training necessarily takes:

1. Preparation to enter the professional schools in theology, medicine, and law, or the graduate school for advanced study in preparation for teaching in college, or research work.

2. Undergraduate professional training in engineering, agriculture, commerce, nursing, pharmacy, architecture, forestry, home economics, fine arts, library science, music, veterinary medicine, and other fields.

3. Preparation for teaching in the grades, or high school.

4. Basic training in cultural and scientific and economic subjects designed to fit a student to enter on an apprenticeship in business or industry.

In an earlier section the placement service of a college was discussed. Its work will be much more effective if graduates are prepared for something. A considerable proportion of the graduates of every liberal arts college will enter graduate courses in law, medicine, theology, or education, or a graduate school for further preparation to teach in a college. Are such of your graduates as do go on with graduate work prepared for it and successful in such work? Are those who graduate in professional courses offered by your college, successful in the practice of the profession for which your college trained them? If some did not succeed, was their failure due to poor teaching in the college; to poorly organized curriculum; to unwisely training students in a field already overcrowded; or to accepting for admission to the course individuals incompetent by preparation and interest or unsuited in personality? If those seeking to teach fail of employment, is it the result of poor teaching, lack of adequate practice teaching facilities, or of inferior ability or personality of the student?

If the graduates of your college cannot make a living, they can scarcely profit from any cultural training they may have received. A study of the occupational success of each graduate is very rewarding.

Social. Our colleges usually claim to develop their students in such a way through study and association with the faculty and with fellow students, that by the time they are graduated they are socially acceptable among educated men. In spite of this claim many college graduates are by no means as acceptable companions as their diplomas would seem to warrant.

Many of the ablest students entering college today, students intellectually capable of serving later in positions of large responsibility, come from homes so limited economically and socially that these young people need development socially to fit them to rise to their best level of service.

Is your institution doing all it should to enable each graduate to live effectively with his fellows?

A consideration of the following questions may help to answer this question:

1. Does your college give all its students some knowledge of the world and some insight into world affairs? A man can no longer guide his own life intelligently without some knowledge of life outside his country.

2. Do your students acquire at college some understanding of the democratic way of life, of democratic values, and get some experience in democratic living?

Russia and Germany have developed national systems of education designed to effectuate national aims. We do not want a federally guided and controlled education. Our system has developed from the bottom. Starting as the elementary school for pioneers on the frontier, as the frontier moved from the Atlantic to the Pacific, the common school served all, rich and poor. As settlements stabilized, schools improved. High schools developed. All followed a common pattern. All were local in support and control. Our colleges developed in much the same way. They developed in a democratic way. Today we tend to forget much of this. We take freedom and democracy for granted. We forget our past struggles to win them, and that they can again be lost. Our teaching of the democratic way of government has become largely formal and unimpressive. With schools and universities enrolling thousands and counting teachers by hundreds, their administration often ceases to set an example of democratic methods and procedures. We must earnestly endeavor to keep the democratic way of life before our youth, both by vivid precept and example of effective operation.

Is the democratic way of life emphasized in your courses in the social and humane studies?

Is the administration of your college democratic, and is the life of the institution among faculty and students permeated with the democratic spirit?

3. Does the college improve the health and sound physical development of all its students? Does it give all fine ideals of

health, physique, and recreation, or does it expend all its money and interests on 200 major athletes for intercollegiate competition? Does every graduate go out with a sound body and robust health so far as his physical endowments permit? Is his physical endowment as he leaves college all that he will need to render the service for which he has been trained?

4. Does your college fully recognize and seriously endeavor to meet its responsibility to develop high ideals of character, and religion in its students? Do students go out with sound character, and with a religious grounding such as to enable them to meet the trials of life and render their greatest service?

5. Do all graduates leave college with a sound rudimentary philosophy of life on which they can build safely as wider experience of life gives them material? Do the content of the college courses, the methods of instruction, and the character and personality of the teachers all tend to help the students formulate a sound philosophy of life? If there is a chapel service, does it make a real contribution to this end? If there are courses in philosophy and psychology, do they make a positive contribution to the building of a sound philosophy of life by the students?

Is your college pursuing the cultural, vocational, and social aims common to all colleges, wisely, and in the best balance for its largest service?

CHAPTER 21

THE COLLEGE AND THE INDIVIDUAL

HOW effectively is your institution serving each individual student? What are the factors that make the college education of an individual worthwhile? A great many students seem to profit but little from their college course. Why? Could it be true at your college?

Assuming that all the students at your college have selected their college wisely, they are not all alike in their individual needs or aims. Every college is today a very complex organization, designed to render a large variety of services. Is your college properly staffed and well organized to serve each student so that his education there will be most worthwhile to him and to our country?

There is much talk in every college about the individual, but with increasing complexity within institutions, and with increasing numbers of students, one finds much evidence that the education of a majority of students is less worthwhile than the generous facilities of our colleges would seem to warrant. There is an increasing tendency to disregard individual differences and treat all very much alike. Curricula and courses are too often shaped to suit professorial convenience and departmental ambition. Variations from regularity are regarded as undesirable. There is a great tendency to shape all to a common form. The able are crowded into it and the weak are stretched to fill it as best may be.

The individual personality is the most precious thing in the world. The college does not do its job well unless it gets behind the reserve of each student; discovers his strengths and weaknesses, his hopes, ambitions, and aims; and so far as possible develops and guides them in such a manner as to enrich and strengthen and bring to full flower the noblest personality that is in him. This is most desirable but very difficult.

The following questions relative to your college will tend to show where its services to the individual are most satisfactory, and where least satisfactory. The following questions refer to each individual student:

1. *Who knows him?* A parent is entitled to assurance that someone in authority in the college will really become acquainted with his son or daughter. Someone worthwhile on the staff, who has understanding and sympathy and high scholarly ideals should certainly be acquainted personally and rather intimately with each student.

2. *What is usefully known of his background?* Much is recorded on papers and cards, filed here and there. Much is often available, but how much about his background is at the finger-ends of the faculty persons responsible for knowing and guiding him?

3. *What is known of his ability to do college work?* Did he do creditably in high school—graduate in the upper quarter, or at least in the upper half of his class? What is his scholastic aptitude score? Does it warrant expectation of success in college? If these indications are unpromising, are there definite reasons to think the student's determination to succeed is great enough to surmount all handicaps? If not, why has he been admitted to a college course which he is probably unable to complete? After he has been in college for one or two quarters, if he shows by his work lack of reasonable promise of success, due to inability, lack of interest, or other cause, is he dropped promptly or retained in class as a burden to the teacher and competent classmates and at a disadvantage to himself? Or, if he is retained, are courses provided for his ability and such as will be truly useful to him?

4. *What is known of his vocational aims, and whether they are suited to his abilities?* If his aims seem reasonable and if he is doing creditable work, all is well. If not, much can be learned through generally accepted tests which will give helpful guidance. Are these tests given to students whose vocational aims seem questionable?

5. *Is this the best college for him all considered?* Certainly the college is for the boy and not the boy for the college. Every college has its strength and its limitations. After becoming acquainted with this boy, his abilities and aims, are the proper authorities satisfied that this college can serve him well? If not, have they told him so and discussed with him other colleges that might serve him better? If not, why not?

6. *Is he enrolled carefully each term in the best courses for him to pursue, all things considered?* Or is he registered in a routine way by an uninterested official, drafted for service on registration day? While the curricula provided by the faculty are usually well planned to serve the average, capable student, they do not usually serve well either the very superior student or the student much below the average. Are the true interests and needs of the student, or conformity to a rigid prescription, most important at your college?

7. *What about his health?* Is each student given a physical examination by a competent physician? Are all doubtful cases followed by further examinations and conferences? Are any weaknesses pointed out and talked over in a helpful way? Are further physical examinations given each year? Is it certain that adequate health measures of all kinds are taken and that each student graduating is in the best health possible considering his condition on admission?

8. *Is he in suitable sports and are any defects in posture or physical development being corrected by suitable exercises?* A student's sound physical development and his fine sense of sportsmanship are most important. Is your college doing all it should to develop

them? Are you offering facilities for a wide enough variety of sports to interest all students, the strong and the frail? Or are all your physical education efforts directed toward turning out winning teams and earning large gate receipts?

9. *Is his social life at college such as to develop him to suitably fill the type of position he should later occupy?* Life in a dormitory or fraternity house can be such as to make a real contribution to the social development of the residents. Are your dormitories and fraternities so run? What is being done for the social development of those living in rooming houses? A very able man, qualified by training and ability for large service, can be greatly handicapped by lack of social experience.

Does the social example of members of the faculty tend to develop the best social ideals and practices in the students?

10. *Is he adequately housed and fed and has he sufficient resources for his minimum needs?* Are the housing and boarding facilities available to students good and reasonably priced? If not, why not? Are students, with inadequate funds allowed to ruin their health in pursuit of an education? Aid should be available to help those of real ability who need help.

11. *If he is earning part or all his expenses, are his labor for support and his college work so balanced that he is profiting the most possible under all circumstances?* A surprising proportion of college students earn all their expenses, and a great many earn part. Students differ greatly in stamina, resourcefulness, and rapidity in learning. Many attempt too much and in the end neither earn a comfortable living nor make creditable grades. Certainly all such should be protected from injuring their health, or needlessly failing in college, by a reduction in college work carried, to such amount as can be carried profitably with the necessary labor load. At Berea College, where all students labor, 60 hours is regarded as a maximum week's work, and no

student is permitted to enter upon a course of study and a labor load which combined require over 60 hours a week.

12. *Is he growing in integrity, in dependability—in every aspect of character—at your college, so that on graduation you can conscientiously recommend him as a man?* Are all the professors and instructors at your college men of high character, men who set a fine example before your students? Are the regulations of the college such as to maintain a fine type of student life? Is the standard of honesty in all classwork and in examinations high? Do the fraternities maintain high standards of character? Does the general temper of classroom instruction tend to build up high standards of character? Are all administrative and official actions of the college on a high level of honor and integrity such as will tend to give a high value to nobility of character on the campus?

13. *Has he grown in his religious life, and is his religious anchorage stronger than when he entered college?* Is the religious attitude of the members of the faculty wholesome? Are lectures and all teaching friendly and cordial to true religious faith? Are the churches stimulating and helpful to students? Are courses that are given in psychology, philosophy, and religion such as to build up rather than to tear down religious faith?

14. *Has he grown in culture, in breadth of knowledge, in appreciation of the beautiful in art, music, and literature, and has a foundation been laid on which further growth can be expected to fit him for his future position in life?* Does his curriculum demand some breadth of education? Is his interest stimulated outside of vocational lines? Is there a cultural atmosphere about the college that contributes to this side of the student's life?

15. *Does the college follow each graduate out into the world and aid him in securing his first job, or in entering on his graduate or professional course?* The college and university graduates many students yearly at large cost. Each graduate should surely be worth placing in a suitable position to begin his service

to the public and the world. It is certainly an important duty of the college to assist her graduates to their first appointment. Does your college do this well?

While no college could answer all the above questions favorably, not one of them is unreasonable. Each individual student should be served as suggested above. While consideration of the questions may lead to the discovery of some special weaknesses in your college, as a whole they go to emphasize what a difficult and many-sided undertaking college education really is. Nowhere is it perfectly done. In no place is every individual properly served. Every institution has far to go to reach even acceptable excellence.

It remains the high duty of each trustee and of each administrative officer to see that his institution has moved forward toward greater perfection of service, and not backward, during the period of his responsibility.

SECTION V

The Duties and Services of Trustees

CHAPTER 22

THE DUTIES AND SERVICES OF TRUSTEES

THE duties and services of trustees are of three kinds: (1) things not to do; (2) duties as one of the board in meetings and committees; and (3) duties as an individual representing the institution to the public.

One of the first things that should be impressed on a new trustee is that he is a trustee and not an executive. The operation of the institution and the selection of the staff are functions of the president and faculty. Trustees are continually besought to secure jobs, contracts, and the retention of dismissed students. All such requests should be referred to the president without recommendation. If the president fails to direct the institution in an effective and satisfactory manner, by all means replace him as soon as possible with a more capable man. But do not assume any personal part in the immediate direction of the college.

As a member of the board and of committees of the board, several responsibilities devolve on a trustee:

1. To become familiar as soon as possible with the buildings, grounds, and equipment, their condition of repair and general suitability to the uses they serve.

2. To become acquainted with the president, deans, and as many of the faculty as possible, that he may form an intelligent estimate of the quality of the personnel and their spirit.

3. To become acquainted, at least superficially with the printed matter issued by the institution. The catalogue, reports, publicity material, and any regular publications of a scholarly type.

4. To assure himself that all endowment funds are safely

and wisely handled and are fully protected in every possible way.

5. To assure himself that all current income and expenditure is handled with absolute integrity and with skill and that all interests of the institution are conserved.

6. To assure himself that the budget is honestly and competently prepared; that income estimates are conservative and expenditures carefully and fully estimated; that all educational needs—salaries, salary increases, new appointments, library, supplies, and equipment—have been carefully considered.

7. To familiarize himself with the fixed policies of the institution; to be active in codifying and adding to these policies, where changes are needed.

8. To assure himself that the president is following the general policies of the trustees in the direction of the institution.

As an individual representing the institution to the public in his area, the trustee has further opportunities to serve most usefully. While there never was a time when as much was spent on higher education by the public, or when so large a number of students attended the undergraduate, professional, and graduate colleges, there seems to be less intimate understanding and sympathy between the public and the colleges than formerly—certainly less than there should be.

The trustee might well be an active intermediary in many ways between his community and his college:

a. In directing qualified high school graduates to his college and in discouraging unqualified graduates from entering.

b. In keeping in touch with the student attitudes in the college through continued acquaintance with the boys and girls who attend his college from his town.

c. In bringing properly selected faculty members before question-asking groups in his community for discussions or lectures.

d. In giving publicity through local newspaper editors relative to worthwhile matters at the college. The community should feel that the trustee is its representative at the college. He should strengthen the relations of the college in serving the public in his community.

e. He should have an interest in the product of his college, and especially in the graduates who went to the college from his town. How has the college changed the boy or girl? Have they grown as men and women? Are they competent in the field of their special training? Can the trustee be proud of the finished product of his college?

The alumni secretary can be a great help in supplying desired information relative to students and graduates from a trustee's home town. Nothing could be more stimulating to an alumni secretary than inquiries from trustees. The alumni monthly, or quarterly, often gives illuminating sketches of the college and its work. The alumni secretary has, or can readily obtain, the latest information on the employment of graduates.

f. So far as may be he should try personally and through the board as a whole, to narrow the gap between trustees and faculty. This gap has always been wide. Half a century ago it was still usual for each professor to report in person to the trustees on his department and submit to questions from trustees. Such meetings were of small value. The faculty is usually doubtful of the competency of the trustees, and the trustees are often critical of the faculty. Anything that brings faculty members and trustees in personal contact improves this situation and is to be desired. Trustees brought in to address faculty groups, and faculty members invited by trustees to address groups in the trustee's community are most useful methods of promoting better acquaintance. A joint committee of trustees and faculty, the latter members elected by the faculty to represent them, can discuss certain common problems with great mutual profit.

This business of being a college trustee can be a great

business, a great pleasure, and a great service. It can also be a very small, useless, and perfunctory performance. A shocking percentage of the 17,000 men and women serving as trustees, directors, and members of the boards controlling our American colleges and universities know little of their responsibilities and care little about their institutions, perfunctorily attend board meetings, and approve presidential recommendations without understanding or serious consideration. On the other hand, there is no finer or more valuable group of people in the country than our able, responsible college trustees. And there are no more rewarding services in which to work. The effective trustee renders an unpaid service of which he may well be proud. To be an active, useful, stimulating factor in the life of a great institution; actively to help unite the administration, the trustees, the faculty, the alumni, and the students in a drive toward noble goals in education; to feel that you are a useful factor in developing the best that is in American youth—all this can mean much in the life of a man. No public trust today is more important than the trusteeship of American colleges and universities.